THE CHALLENGE OF MARRIAGE

THE CHALLENGE
OF MARRIAGE

by

RUDOLF DREIKURS, M.D.

Hawthorn/Dutton
New York

THE CHALLENGE OF MARRIAGE

ISBN: 0-8015-1177-1

7   8   9   10

PREFACE TO THE NEW EDITION

SINCE the publication of this book, certain trends, suggested then, are now a commonplace on our contemporary scene. The conflicts and tensions that disrupt the harmony and even threaten the survival of individual marriages have increased in frequency and intensity.

However, our American family is not disintegrating, despite all its shortcomings. It is true that sexual satisfaction is lacking in many marriages; and they often fail to provide the proper stimulation and guidance for children to grow and mature socially, emotionally, and intellectually. Since these are considered as two crucial functions in marriage, many begin to question the usefulness of this institution. This seems to be unwarranted.

We suggest that the family is not disintegrating, but is rather faced with a serious dilemma. It is the result of the democratic evolution with its concomitant process of equalization. Tradition has not prepared us for it. We do not know how to resolve conflicts and clashes of interests in the spirit of mutual respect, a prerequisite for living in a democratic atmosphere. Our cultural inability to live with each other as equals, which we have become in fact, is most painfully felt in our closest relationship, in marriage.

One of the significant changes that became more evident in the last decade is the trend toward a new pattern of femininity. It has far-reaching consequences for the relationship of women to men and children. There are exceptions, but women, by and large, are no longer trying to establish their equality with men by imitating them. When this book was first published, the tendency of women to accept heretofore specifically masculine patterns was noted. It was at a time when masculine superiority was still widely recognized—and challenged. Today the situation is quite different. Women no longer look up to men, although they often wish they could. It has become much more customary for men to look up to women. One can hardly see any family where father still knows best; but mother usually does.

American women try so hard to be "good." One has to define what this goodness means. It is no longer purity, chastity, and virtue, traditionally expected and demanded from women. Women do not want necessarily to be chaste; but even in their sexual freedom and license, they want to be proper. Being proper, socially correct, irreproachable, becomes a widely accepted ideal for women. Women have become the arbiters and censors, the custodians of morals and mores, imposing their rules of proper conduct on men and on society as a whole. The sexual mores of this country will greatly depend on the attitudes and conventions that women will develop and establish. At the present time they either try to impose on men the demand for fidelity and chastity, previously only required of women; or they arrogate to themselves the same license and sexual freedom that men enjoyed throughout the ages.

In the past men, in exclusive possession of political and social power, established the social conventions to their liking and benefit, and women had to conform and to abide by the rigid demands for chastity. Today virtue is *their* right, *their* prerogative. During the last decade very few men sought marital consultation because their wives did not behave properly; such complaints on the part of the husbands had been the rule in the past. Today the wives complain that their husbands do not behave properly, in a socially acceptable way. They either are too passive, aloof, and withdrawn, or too aggressive and domineering. Rarely do we see a husband who can tell his wife what is proper; she usually tells him. This desire of women to be perfect, to be right, leaves neither husbands nor children a chance to be good enough. An increasing number of boys grow up with the mistaken conviction that in order to be a real man one has to be "bad" or fight. Previously men had to be reliable, reasonable, strong, and trustworthy, while women were supposed to be weak, soft, emotional, and, therefore, unstable and unpredictable. To a certain extent we even witness an opposite tendency as to what constitutes a man and what a woman. Instead of a picture of the superior male, there is the incipient cultural image of the superior woman. This does not mean that we are in danger of becoming a matriarchal society. In the process of the democratic evolution there is no prospect of any group setting itself up permanently as superior. The confusion and vacillation is merely the result of the democratic changes, of our groping for a new relationship, which eventually will be based on equal status for all.

The second trend that has become more pronounced in the last decade is the emancipation of children. It is becoming increasingly obvious that adults have lost their power and authority over children, who have gained a sense of freedom and self-determination. But while children became free to do as they decide, they often do not develop a sense of responsibility. Freedom without responsibility can be a considerable social threat. Many parents became permissive, out of a sincere desire not to be autocratic. The consequences of a general overpermissiveness are becoming painfully obvious. We witness a trend to revert to strictness and severity as a means of stemming the tide of juvenile unruliness and rebellion. However, neither permissiveness nor strictness can solve the problem. Parents need new approaches that would enable them to become a match for their children, to deal with them as equals, with mutual respect.

Without knowledge and skill in coping with each other in a democratic atmosphere our families become a battleground, torn by tensions, antagonisms, and hostilities. Husbands and wives find it difficult to get along peacefully. Under the impact of the ensuing warfare in which the children fully participate, their marital relationship can often be strained to the breaking point. Instead of being an element of unification, children often become an almost unsolvable disrupting influence.

This book has attempted to outline the new approaches in marital relationships that the democratic atmosphere of our country requires. It suggests how people can live with each other as equals. It intends to provide a guide through the maze of the social tensions with which a new society is engulfed and which characterize our era of transition from an autocratic past into a democratic future.

Chicago   R. D.

CONTENTS

THE CHALLENGE OF MARRIAGE

CONTENTS

INTRODUCTION

WRITING a book on marriage imposes great responsibilities on the author. Much has been written and much has been read about sex and marriage, not always with benefit to the reader. Far too often people use reading and thinking about their problems to avoid doing anything about them.

But reading with critical evaluation can serve another purpose. It can be an organized examination of premises with a view to finding constructive solutions for problems. It is this type of reading which this book hopes to stimulate.

All problems in love, sex, and marriage may be regarded as the expression of social, cultural, political, economic, and psychological processes converging upon the individual. Only through understanding these processes can we find orientation for actions in solving these problems. The background of the writer predisposes him to an emphasis upon psychological mechanisms. However, no psychological investigation can overlook those sociological and cultural conditions which affect the individual and are responsible for his problems. This book aims to integrate sociological and psychological approaches.

Throughout this book the reader will feel the marked influence of the thinking of Alfred Adler. For several reasons the writer has chosen Adler's Individual Psychology as the basis for understanding human nature.

First of all, Adler's interpretation of the individual personality, his recognition of a distinct life style in each individual, offers one of the best psychological techniques available today. As the style of life represents the fundamental and all-embracing outlook of each person on life in general, so the recognition of the resultant personal goals and attitudes provides a basis for understanding all actions, thoughts, and emotions.

The second reason for using Adler's psychology is its constructiveness and optimism. In contrast to other psychologists, Adler sees life as an unceasing development, not merely as a futile activity leading to death and final destruction. Only in such light can we comprehend the evolution of mankind and the progress that has been made and must still be continued.

The third benefit in using Individual Psychology is the concurrence of its observations and findings with present trends in social and political sciences. Adler's psychology emphasizes the significance of personal interrelationships; it serves better than any other psychology I know for the understanding and solution of social problems—and all human problems are essentially social problems; for no problem affects only one person alone. And certainly the problems of sex and marriage require two to work toward a solution.

If the process of understanding, of clarification and encouragement, which this book attempts to stimulate, leads to improvement, development and constructive action, the purpose of this book will be well served.

THE CHALLENGE OF MARRIAGE

I.

WHAT IS LOVE?

WE *do* know love. Every generation has had its poets and singers to praise it, its cynics and misanthropes to attack it, and its psychologists and philosophers to explain it. No one denies that love *is*. We argue only about *what* love is. For there are as many definitions of love as there are lovers.

Why then, if love is so well known, is there such complete disagreement concerning its nature? Does love reveal itself in different garb to each observer? Does it vary with the age or the culture in which a man lives? Or does it perhaps change with the sex, age, or amorous experience of the lover? (Or, for that matter, of the interpreter of love?)

In examining love as well as in inquiring into the nature of any other human phenomenon, one must examine both the psychological and sociological aspect of the problem. The psychological aspect involves the personal attitudes and aims of the individual, which are based upon the intellectual and emotional development of his personality. The sociological aspect involves the social concepts and conventions of the community of which the individual is

3

a part. An objective evaluation of the problem of love must include both aspects. In this chapter we will deal with the psychological aspect of love.

Psychologically, since love is considered one of the emotion complexes, we may proceed by examining first the general characteristics of emotion and then the specific characteristics of the emotion of love.

THE FUNCTION OF EMOTIONS

Emotion is generally considered as caused by some environmental situation. The individual subjected to a certain stimulation is supposed automatically to react with the emotion corresponding to the situation. For example, in the infant, the stimulus of loud noise (like thunder) or the stimulus of loss of support may evoke the reaction of fear. The whole elaborate structure of adult fear is supposed to be erected upon such primitive stimulus-response mechanisms. The theory that human behavior is mainly based on such stimulus-response mechanisms is widely accepted today.

According to the Freudian [1] theory, all fears can be traced back to the "psychic trauma" of being born, the "primary anxiety" experienced by every individual during his passage from the warmth and security of his mother's body into a cold world. Freud also advances the theory that fears and anxiety are caused by the suppression of sexual excitement which is not permitted to take its normal course.[1]

Such concepts, interesting and correct as they may be, are inadequate in explaining the real function of fear. It is

[1] Sigmund Freud, *Introductory Lectures to Psychoanalysis*. Boni & Liveright, New York, 1920.

4

obvious that the individual needs the emotion of fear for biological or psychological reasons. It serves a purpose, namely, that of avoiding dangers or unpleasant situations. Regarding fear from a teleological or purposive point of view is helpful not only in gaining a better understanding of the psychological mechanisms involved; it also provides a better approach for helping the individual to understand his fears and to deal with them sensibly. The purpose of fear might not be easily recognized, especially if common sense and logic do not justify the fear, as in cases of imaginary dangers and unreasonable emotional anxieties. A careful psychological study of such instances reveals nevertheless a very definite purpose motivating the individual to take a defensive attitude against a situation which may imply dangers not only to his physical well-being, but more often to his prestige and social status.

All emotions are directed toward specific goals, even if these goals in adults are not obvious but concealed by an elaborate psychological superstructure. Emotions are actively selected by the individual. It is difficult to perceive this fact, because emotions cannot serve well if and when recognized in their purposiveness. Therefore, it is psychologically necessary that one does not admit to oneself one's own control over one's own emotions. Emotions prepare, support, or reject actions. Every action is the result of intellectual and emotional motivations. In thinking, we consider both the pros and cons of the future action. Reason and logic permit and even demand the recognition of advantages and obstacles to any action. However, often enough the decision is difficult to make, as the pros and cons almost equal up. In order to move in any one direc-

5

tion, we must strengthen the apparent value of the direction we favor. It is here that we call upon our emotions. We need emotions to justify our decision and to meet the obstacles which logically might deter us from our chosen course. Without emotions we could not act forcefully. We, therefore, select those emotions which are appropriate to the maintenance and strengthening of our fundamental direction in life.

LOVE AS AN EMOTION

Let us now turn to the consideration of love. Is love, like fear, an emotion with a purpose? There are certainly many general prejudices against this idea. We have been taught from early childhood that love is what *happens* to an individual when he meets the "right" object of his devotion. The cloak of mystery with which love has become invested has been maintained by most of our literature, our movies, and the other arts. We speak of "falling in love" and "falling out of love" in almost the same sense of unexpected, unexplainable coincidence as we would speak of falling over an unseen object. Indeed, it often appears to us as just such an accident. We speak glibly of love as being eternal, unrequited, unfortunate, adolescent, all encompassing, or blind, as though there were different types of love instead of merely different types of lovers. Can it be that love is the result of some mysterious influence that *acts upon* two people whom good fortune has thrown together? Are we in fact merely the passive agents of love?

Let us confine our inquiry temporarily to the sexual drive, which has been considered the least "manageable" element in the emotion-complex we call love. If we can show that even fundamental organic sexuality is under our control, that we use it to suit our purpose, perhaps we can accept more easily the idea of the purposive nature of love itself.

THE FUNCTION OF SEXUALITY

It has long been our unfortunate practice to explain human sexuality by analogy with animal sexuality. Even our linguistic habits bear this out when we consider the use of the terms wolf, (gay) dog, lion (with women), bull, the Old English cuckold (cf. cuckoo), the Spanish *cabron*, and bitch in many languages. We seem ever ready to account for (and to blame and excuse) our sexual behavior in terms of a primitive, instinctual, animal-like drive, over which we exert a degree of "control," depending upon the extent to which we are "civilized." This is a very comfortable type of rationalization, if only we can forget certain biological facts:

> First: Animal sexuality is limited in specie and sex. This is not true in human sexuality. One has merely to cite the examples of sodomy and homosexuality to prove this point.
> Second: Animal sexuality is limited by *time* through the oestrus cycle in the female. That is, the female is ready for love only when in heat. And the male is aroused exclusively by the covetous female. The adult human, however, is always biologically ready for sexual activity.
> Third: Animal sexuality is limited by the necessary presence and function of the sex glands. Castration

7

produces a neuter or sexless animal. The human being may undergo removal of ovaries or testes after puberty with little change in sexuality. He is capable of sexual excitement before his sex glands mature in puberty, and after they cease to function at the climacteric.

Fourth: Animal-sexuality is characterized not only by limitation but also by compulsion. Once the male is aroused, he must perform and can be stopped only by physical force.

One may, of course, dispute these facts with evidence from the observations of the sexual behavior of certain animals. But it should be noted that those animals which, in regard to sex, behave more like human beings, are affected by conditions similar to those which are characteristic for humans, namely, by close social relationships. Domestic animals and animals living in close groups deviate in many regards from other species. The greatest deviations from sexual limitations and compulsions are found in organisms living in closest group formations, namely, bees and ants. These have reached a point of almost complete mastery of sex. They, by their own efforts, can determine which offspring will be male and which female and, as a lone exception in the animal kingdom, they can even produce sexless beings (worker bees), merely by dietary methods.

The primates, apes and monkeys, behave sexually much like human beings. Their sexuality, like that of human beings, is not limited to specific periods. Their freedom from cyclicity is regarded as the result of a tendency to gain dominance by sexual aggression—a motivation that is independent of any hormonally determined sexual behavior.[2] Since the dominance drive is active at all times, sexual behavior is observed in these animals at any time of the sexual cycle. According to the same source, homosexual behavior in monkeys is not a sexual abnormality or perversion. In most cases it has nothing to do with sex drive. It is an expression of dominance and submission, and sexual gender makes no difference in dominance behavior.

It is apparent that we humans also are neither limited nor compelled in the expression of sexuality by the biologic needs of our bodies. As we learned to control nature around us, so we became independent of natural urges within ourselves. Sexually we are polymorphous—capable of heterosexual, homosexual, and autosexual behavior at almost any age and no matter what the state of our sex glands. And we can refrain from any sex activity if we so choose.

Many theories have been advanced to explain how the fundamental biologic sexual drive is modified in human beings. We can find one idea held in common by the proponents of most of these theories. They feel that somewhere along the course of development of the individual, he is subjected to some experience which shapes the future expression of his sexuality. The experience may be thought of as a psychic trauma which "fixates" his "libido," or as a stimulus which results in the "conditioning" of the "native sex drive." In either case, the individual is thought of as being acted upon by his environment.

This is a very comforting idea. If one accepts it, he is

[2] A. H. Maslow, Individual Psychology and the Social Behavior of Monkeys and Apes. *International Journal of Individual Psychology*, vol. 1, 1935.

9

given theoretical justification for any type of indulgence—the only prerequisite being that he shall have suffered from some sexually "traumatic" experience in his past. (And who hasn't!) The only difficulty is, that of the many individuals exposed to the same sexual experience in childhood and adolescence, only a few will deviate into the sexual perversions, and, of these, no two will show identical patterns of sexual behavior.

SEXUALITY AS A TOOL

It is evident, then, that there must be something else which determines the mode of sexual behavior. Can it be that we, ourselves, choose the form of our own sexual expression? And does this choice reflect our use of sex for a definite purpose? The following case may help answer this question:

Mrs. D., age 54, complained that her husband, who was over 60 years old, was altogether too passionate. While her sexual desires had decreased considerably, Mr. D. approached her almost nightly—even more frequently then he used to. He maintained he could not control his urge and that it was her duty to satisfy it.

Mrs. D. was advised not only to accede to her husband's demands but to appear even more passionate than he and to make even further demands upon him sexually. She accepted this advice, but not without some doubt. She later reported that her change in behavior had completely astonished her husband. At first he didn't know what to do about it. Then, the more she demanded, the more he retreated. Finally he became impotent.

It will be readily seen that in this case we are dealing not alone with the sexual drive. Otherwise, the wife's treatment of her husband would not have resulted in his impotence. Actually the couple was engaged in a competition for dominance, and the husband was using his sexual capacity in his fight for his "rights." The basic marital problem was not sexual and therefore was not solved by the strategy outlined above. But the case affords an example of how sexuality may be *used*. We choose the mode of sexual expression in accordance with the way it serves our fundamental goals.[3]

If we accept this thesis, how can we explain the fact that we don't see the purpose in our own sexual behavior? Can it be that we merely seem to be passive victims of our drives and our emotions because we don't want to admit responsibility for our behavior? As long as our basic intentions conform with our conscience, we accept full responsibility for our actions. But occasionally we can't reconcile intentions with conscience. It is here that we refuse to acknowledge our intentions and resort to the use of emotions to justify our actions. The following case may help illustrate this point:

John B. was deeply "in love." So great was his passion for Alice that he could think of nothing else. Unfortunately, she didn't respond, and she rejected his proposal. But John was the sort of fellow who always got what he wanted. So he pursued her and pleaded his cause persistently. The girl remained obdurate. Then John became desperate and threatened suicide. At this point she weakened, for did this not prove how much he loved her? So she married him.

Now John lost his interest in Alice and neglected her, even sexually. When she complained tearfully that he didn't love her any more, he told her he couldn't help it, for he was no longer in love! Then she divorced him.

[3] "From the way in which a person deals with love and sexual problems one can understand much about his character." Alexandra Adler—*Guiding Human Misfits*. The Macmillan Company, New York, 1938.

Whereupon John "fell in love" with Alice again. He could not live without her. Now he was really in love with her. And he again pursued her but with even greater urgency than before. To escape him, she married someone else.

Now John was really challenged. He was again determined to have Alice for his wife. So he began to threaten the life of her second husband. To protect the latter from John's threats, Alice divorced him. The tempo of John's pursuit now accelerated. He convinced her that his divorce had taught him a lesson, that he needed her, that he was a "changed man," and that his love was now both profound and eternal. So she remarried him.

As one may suspect, it was not long before John again began to neglect his wife. And, of course, it was not his fault. For somehow or other he was again out of love.

It is now apparent that our hero was concerned not with the establishment of a satisfying state of *being* in love, but rather with proving that he could cause a woman to *fall* in love with him whenever he might choose. Once this was accomplished, he was no longer interested in her until his possession of her was again challenged. It was not love, but his desire to put a woman into his service that motivated him. How convenient it was to attribute this fluctuation in his interest to the notorious undependability of the emotion of love!

We come now to the discussion of the emotion-complex we call love. Can we show that we ourselves determine the direction, and even the very existence of love? Do we use love as we use sex to serve our fundamental purposes?

THE FUNCTION OF ROMANCE

In our days the goals of love are often peculiar. This is attested to by the relatively infrequent attainment of the goal which each individual sets for himself. How many of

12

us actually find what we conceive to be complete happiness in love? How many more have reconciled themselves unwillingly to their disappointment in love? What of those who are unhappily waiting for love to *happen* to them? What of those sophisticates who cynically proclaim their discovery that love is a fiction—with the same peculiar mixture of joy and pathos that characterized their earlier announcement of the nonexistence of Santa Claus?

In a way there is much similarity between our concept of love and that of the jolly old man, who, at infrequent intervals, mysteriously enters our home to bring us gifts. We have only to be good and keep our eyes shut in excited expectancy and Santa will arrive in a triumph of tinkling bells, reindeer hoof-beats, and falling snowflakes, to bestow upon us our rewards. Of course, Mr. Claus will omit us if we try to discover how he comes or goes.

Romantic love is a concept hard to give up. We still want to have our hearts stormed by love. We long wistfully to have our souls assaulted and conquered by some mysterious force against which we are powerless. And we are as loath to relinquish this concept as we were to give up the myths of our childhood. For many of us the criterion of true love is that it be spiced with a dash of unhappiness. There should be just the right amount of heartache, sleeplessness, and inability to concentrate on one's work. Add to this just a grain of jealousy (more would spoil the brew) and one has the secret formula for romantic love. Who is there who dares to doubt the value of this formula? Do we not see it proved again and again in the astonishing masterpieces produced in our motion pictures, our radio serials, our magazines, and our Sunday newspaper supplements?

13

How does the sort of love we have compare with that for which we are seeking? How can we be sure that we are really in love unless we continually feel a peculiar sensation in the chest or the abdomen, together with an intense desire to be with the loved one? When we see two people living harmoniously together and showing nothing more than a feeling of devotion, responsibility, and belongingness, we think of them not as lovers but as a "couple." We say that they are no longer in the romantic stage of their love, and maybe we feel just a trifle sorry for them. How much more exciting is the existence of the Don Juan or coquette who collects romances as a hobby—and displays his trophies for the approval of his friends.

There are several well-known phenomena which lead us to the daring suspicion that maybe romance is not what we think it is. Otherwise, it would not lead so often to heartache, misery, and disappointment. Consider the romantic enchantment of unrequited love, or witness what happens occasionally when two brave lovers, facing a world hostile to their union, suddenly find all opposition gone and their love gone with it. Or think how the least desirable types are often the most desired as lovers—no one can expect to be happily married to a Don Juan and yet . . . We may conclude from all these observations that romantic love serves mainly as stimulation to offset common sense and good judgment. This type of emotion seems to be chosen for the purpose of picturing promises which can never be fulfilled in real life. It is a daydream of a discouraged person, who does not believe in his own future happiness and seeks unrealistic pleasures to soften his despair.

Can there be any other kind of love? What would it be

like? Would it repay us for giving up the idea of romantic love?

THE FUNCTION OF LOVE

Love, like any other emotion, always functions in the support of the fundamental aims of an individual. The presence or absence of love, its direction and degree, and its durability depend in any given case upon basic attitudes toward the relationship between the self and the other one. Thus, for the individual with a high degree of social interest, love can be the implement of the greatest contribution he can make to another, the giving of all he has and all he is. It may become the most sincere expression of one's desire to belong.

But in the individual who is deficient in social interest, love can be an instrument of hostility and can subserve the desire to remain outside the community. It is in this abuse of love that we find the passion and even violence which sometimes attend unwise or forbidden love. For strong emotion may be needed to suppress common sense and conscience and to facilitate the rejection of obligations to the community. The greater the opposition to the logic of social life, the more one must find a convincing alibi to justify his defiance. And where can he find a better alibi than in a love in whose presence he is helpless?

If we acknowledge that we choose the direction of our love in accordance with our fundamental purposes, it can be said that we even decide upon whether or not to fall in love. Of course, this decision is one of which we are usually unaware.

The realization of being in love is a moment of high importance psychologically. It is characterized by a desire to give oneself and to accept the other one, by a sustained and exclusive interest in the other one, by a longing to be together.

The existence of love is threatened whenever our attitude toward the other one changes. When our social interest diminishes through some deep discouragement, we become sensitive to influences which we formerly ignored. It is here that we find a slight tarnish in the love dream and begin to look for that degree of perfection which is worthy of our love.

Thus, love depends upon the intentions of the lover. If these are directed toward cooperation in mutual achievement, love can be a blessing which may give articulate expression to the poetry inherent in every soul. If they represent a discouragement and distrustful withdrawal from participation, love can be the devil's own instrument for destroying duty and decency. "Only a courageous human being is capable of experiencing real love." [4]

LOVE AS ONE OF THE THREE LIFE TASKS

What love means to an individual depends therefore upon how he uses love in regard to his entire life situation. Love is a task which confronts every human being as a part of human society. There is a definite interrelationship between the task of love and the two other life tasks, namely, to work, and to get along socially with other human beings. Success in life means solving these three problems. They all demand social feeling and courage, and

[4] Erwin Wexberg, *The Psychology of Sex*. Farrar & Rinehart, New York, 1931.

16

readiness for cooperation. A good husband generally makes a good worker and a good friend. On the other hand, he who runs away from love and marriage is a coward and probably retreats also in other spheres of his social life.

This interaction among the three life problems can, however, also take a contradictory turn. It is possible to use one obligation against the others. One can become so entangled in love that he has neither time nor a clear head for work. He misuses his love against his other life problems. Or he may become exclusively interested in his work in order to avoid any relationship with the opposite sex or social contact. Love can be misused against life in a thousand ways. Even very happy marriages are occasionally based on the anti-social desires of two individuals to avoid social integration. And in the realm of love itself, one component of love can be used to destroy the other: sexual attraction for one person might be put in opposition to the understanding and companionship of another person. Through either method a harmonious union is prevented, although the "feeling" of love seems to be experienced in either case.

DEFINITION OF LOVE

Now it is clear why no satisfactory answer has been given to the question, "What is Love?" From a scientific point of view, we have to include in the term love all the emotional attractions between two persons of the opposite sex, from the slightest amount of sympathy to the deepest devotion, with or without obvious sexual desire. But we also have to include every kind of sexual attraction regardless of the object, be it a person of the opposite sex or not. This broad concept has, of course, little value for any practical application. There is no possibility of deciding objectively which love is true, which insincere; which one is real, which imaginary. Love as an emotion is highly subjective. Love is what one calls love—and one calls love any strong emotion of desire, be it created for devotion or domination, for heaven or hell, for happiness or misery.

In order to understand why so many people misuse or do not use at all their "natural" ability for loving, why so many are disappointed and unhappy, and why harmonious and satisfactory marriages seem to become more and more an exception, we have to look for social factors. Then we can expect an answer to the undeniable fact that most of us lack confidence in ourselves and in others, without which constructive love is impossible. Apparently, we are not ready for love. And what many call love is certainly not what love could be.

II.

THE WAR BETWEEN THE SEXES

LOVE FRUSTRATIONS—A SOCIAL PROBLEM

Millions of people suffer from love, millions are stricken by the plague of jealousy, disappointed and disgusted with their mates, unhappy in a joyless marriage, or lonely and loveless in empty solitude. This situation cannot be explained as due simply to the maladjustments of some individuals. Whenever a problem concerns a large part of the population, we must look for deeper causes, either in the structure of society, or in other unfortunate circumstances which in various degree affect all alike.

Thus, the individual man or woman acts as representative of his sex. The marital troubles of Mr. X. and the friction between Joan and her boy friend become, by their identity with the problems of thousands of other men and women, a characteristic sign of a general conflict between the sexes. Even those who deny the existence of a so-called war between the sexes cannot avoid being involved themselves. Others who are aware of it rarely recognize the real reason for this war. Does it arise from the natural biological and psychological differences between man and woman?

19

Or is it caused by the general tension in our present social life?

There seems to be a "natural" antagonism between man and woman, which has caused friction and warfare where-ever there have been men and women. "Lovesickness," jealousy, and adultery are as old as the human race. But their frequency and implications vary. We have good reason to believe that in past generations—let us say one or two hundred years ago—men and women were more satis-fied and closer to each other than we find them today. To-day, sexual dissatisfaction and marital maladjustment are more frequent than ever, with significant differences in the conflicts observed in various countries and nations. Super-ficially, it might look as if racial or geographical factors determine these differences. Marital problems in Anglo-Saxon countries differ from those in Latin countries, those in Europe from those in China, those among Christians from those among Mohammedans; but, on comparing these differences, we come to realize that one factor is every-where of decisive importance in determining the nature and type of the problem: the position of woman in the respec-tive societies. And further, any intensification or alarming increase in the frequency of marital discord coincides with a conspicuous change in the social relationship of the sexes.

THE SOCIAL POSITION OF WOMEN

Today, even while we watch, the social position of women is altering; and we must understand the nature and direc-tion of these changes in order to evaluate properly their implications. Obviously, woman is no longer as dependent upon man as she once was, and she enjoys more rights now

than ever before. Many men and even women who un-
waveringly believe in masculine superiority regard this independence of women as the cause of every evil. They are
convinced that happiness in marriage would be regained,
peace between the sexes restored, if women were restored
to their position of semi-slavery, without the social, sexual,
and professional liberties which they enjoy today. The advocates of this idea believe in the biological inferiority of
women and regard the present growing equality between
the sexes as unnatural and disastrous. They refer to the physical shortcomings of women in stature and muscular capacity and, in particular, look upon the comparative small-
ness of the feminine brain as sufficient proof of the natural
designation of women as subordinate beings. Moebius [1]
spoke of the "physiological imbecility" of women; and
"Thou goest to women? Do not forget thy whip!" is the
advice of the philosopher who worshiped the "Superman"
(Nietzsche, *Thus Spake Zarathustra*). More recently, the
German anthropologist Waldeyer [2] stated that, "A wide
collation of measurements and statistics proves that she
(woman) has a smaller brain, less physical strength, preserves more traits of infancy and childhood in adult life,
etc. Therefore, . . . all efforts to establish entire equality
between the two sexes and to throw open to women all the
avenues of activities enjoyed by men, are mistaken and
will prove failures."

History, however, proves this conception of feminine in-

[1] Paul Julius August Moebius, *Über den Physiologischen Schwachsinn
des Weibes*. C. Marhold, Halle, 1901.
[2] Waldeyer, The Somatic Differences of the Two Sexes. Open address
to the German Society of Anthropology at Essen, 1944. *Science*, vol. 103,
1946.

feriority to be unjustified. The advocates of this doctrine deny or do not know that women were not always the subordinate sex.

THE CONFUSION OF THE MALE SCIENTIST

Mankind has gone through cultural periods where women were dominant. Unfortunately, we have no clear and generally accepted knowledge of the extent and time of feminine dominance called matriarchate. Incredible though it may sound, scientists have often misread the evidence regarding societies ruled by women. The present anarchy of opinion can be explained only by the biased attitudes of the individual scientists toward the problems involved. Contradictions in the interpretations of obvious facts are as old as the differences between matriarchal and patriarchal social organizations. Greek historians describing historical events in Egypt, and Athenians bewildered about the conditions in Sparta, made the same mistakes and committed unintentionally the same falsifications; these men living under masculine hegemony were unable to understand the conditions and customs in a matriarchal society.

That was true then, and it is true today. When Bachofen [3] published his first book on the Mother Rule in 1861, he revealed social relations unrecognized before. The end of the nineteenth century brought forth a great number of scientific publications about matriarchal cultures, describing ancient societies and primitive communities under feminine rule. This sociological research was carried on in a period of growing feminine emancipation. At the beginning of the present century, a complete reversal in the opin-

[3] J. Bachofen, *Das Mutterrecht*. Krais and Hoffmann, Stuttgart, 1861.

22

ions of historians, sociologists, and anthropologists took place. Westermarck [4] was the leading exponent of this change in contemporary thinking. For decades it was considered unscientific in America to talk about matriarchate. Curiously enough, the scientists of Europe, at least before the rise of fascism, did not participate in this retrograde development, and leading sociologists continued to recognize the existence of matriarchal cultures, until the rise of Nazism. [5] Their publications are almost unknown and little quoted in contemporary American research. It took the effort of Robert Briffault [6] to restore scientific dignity to previously ridiculed opinions. Since his public dispute with Westermarck, it is permissible again to talk about matriarchate. [7]

[4] Edward Westermarck, *The History of Human Marriage*. The Macmillan Company, New York, 1921.

[5] Waldeyer (cf. p. 21) states that "woman has practically in all times and places held a position inferior to man."

[6] Robert Briffault, *The Mothers*. The Macmillan Company, New York, 1927.

[7] At the present time most of the leading sociologists and anthropologists still deny that human communities were ever governed by women. R. H. Lowie (*Primitive Society;* Liveright, New York, 1920), widely recognized in the field, states emphatically that "there is no example of true matriarchate" and that women never were the rulers; while Briffault, Mathilde and Mathias Vaerting (*The Dominant Sex;* G. Allen and Unwin, London, 1923), and many others report a great number of scientific findings to the contrary. Lowie and other leading anthropologists disregard ancient societies, some of which had extensive feminine supremacy, like Crete, Sparta, and the early Egypt. They study mainly present primitive societies where there is actually much evidence of typical matriarchal structures—matrilineal kinship, matrilocal residence, avunculate, and similar conditions—which they describe without admitting that these peculiar social privileges of women indicate various degrees and stages of matriarchal rule.

We must agree with Lowie that "social phenomena are not simple, and accordingly the same condition, owing to an indefinite number of unknown concomitants, will produce quite different results in different areas." (In *General Anthropology*, edited by Franz Boas. D. C. Heath & Company,

The reported relationship between the sexes under matriarchate is not only interesting in itself, but gives us important clues for the understanding of the conditions existing today. From our knowledge of matriarchal societies, present conflicts in regard to sex and marriage gain a different aspect. All the characteristic functions and rights of man in our society become recognizable as merely social functions of the dominant sex, while under certain circumstances women did possess all the rights and privileges which are attributed in our present culture to men. "The alleged superiority of man has neither a biological nor

Boston, 1938). The resultant variety of forms and structures should not prevent a recognition of the fundamental basis of all matriarchal phenomena. It seems that the work of Ruth Benedict and especially of Margaret Mead may initiate a new trend of thought in anthropology. Their findings seem to be more in line with our psychological observations of human behavior. "The theories of anthropologists are 'plausible hypotheses,' arrived at after exhaustive studies of widely scattered primitive peoples. But the very diversity of their findings and the resultant contradictory generalizations make one hesitate to give unqualified acceptance to any one theory," says Baber (*Marriage and the Family;* McGraw-Hill, New York, 1939), sizing up the situation. For this reason, it seems that every generalization is unjustifiable, be it an assertion often encountered that matriarchate had always preceded the patriarchal structure of civilized societies, or that true matriarchate had never existed. Under various social conditions, any kind of social organization seems to be possible.

It seems obvious that scientific concepts in regard to matriarchate vary with time and place; opinions accepted here are rejected somewhere else, and what was considered true yesterday appears wrong today and may be recognized as correct again tomorrow. It is an interesting question to consider whether these changes in scientific concepts are produced only by new scientific discoveries which make earlier ones obsolete, or whether they reflect social influences to which the scientist is no less exposed than any other member of a group. Similarly, the contradictory opinions confusing many scientific fields today, as anthropology and sociology, history, psychiatry, and psychology, and even physics, indicate the relativity of any scientific findings, reflecting more the points of view of the individual scientists than absolute truth, which probably does not exist. Could we assume, perhaps, that the confusion among the scientists reflects the confusion of the whole cultural era, of the society in which we live?

24

mental nor psychological basis. Any existing 'superiority is purely a function of economic (we would prefer to say social—R.D.) conditions." [8]

Observations on animals in captivity, living in close group relationships, reveal similar conditions. "Among monkeys the strongest animal governs the cage and does all the sexual mounting. It makes no difference whether the male or the female assumes the role of the dominant animal. If a female is the strongest specimen, she acts sexually exactly as does a male overlord." [9]

THE FOUR RIGHTS OF THE DOMINANT SEX

The superiority of one sex over another may be characterized by certain privileges. These privileges, through which the dominant position of one sex is established in the community, include political, social, economic, and sexual rights.

Until one hundred years ago political rights were exclusively in the hands of men. Women as rulers are rare exceptions in masculine societies, and these exceptions occur only in certain situations in a feudalistic organization. Women certainly were not admitted to minor political and administrative offices.

The social rights were in accordance with political supremacy. Women did not possess any social rights. They derived their social privileges exclusively from the position of husband, father, or brother. The woman's social status changed with that of the man upon whom she depended.

[8] W. Beran Wolfe, A Woman's Best Years. Emerson Books, New York, 1935.
[9] A. H. Maslow. Cf. page 9.

25

Any social position could be obtained through marriage. Alone she was nothing, through the man—anything!

The economic status of a woman was consistent with her social dependency. No economic power was available to her. She could work only for man, either in the household of her own family, or as servant in another. Woman could not inherit or possess property. Her earnings belonged to the master of her family. He alone could hold property, make contracts, sue or be sued.[10]

SPECIFIC SEXUAL RIGHTS

The dominant sex has also certain privileges which may be called sexual rights. It seems difficult to understand what the term sexual rights could mean. Everyone has the "natural" right to marry, the right to love, the right to satisfy his sexual desire. What other sexual rights are conceivable? There are some, to be sure. The manner in which these "natural" rights are used is of utmost significance. Definite rules direct the conduct of each sex. Certain privileges are reserved exclusively for the dominant sex. These privileges, in regard to sexual life, imply *activity* in selecting, approaching, and winning a mate, and also the liberty to be promiscuous.

During the period of extreme masculine dominance, women were merely objects of masculine desire, properties which man could acquire in unrestricted number. It was considered natural for man to be polygamous, while women were strictly compelled to be devoted to one man alone. The Mohammedans and the Chinese, the latter until re-

[10] Ray E. Baber, *Marriage and the Family*. McGraw-Hill, New York, 1939.

26

cently, illustrate the conditions under extreme masculine supremacy.

Under matriarchate the conditions were different.[11] Women possessed political power. They determined the social position for the man whom they married and for their offspring. Men married into the wife's clan and the children inherited the mother's name. At times, the socially valued professions were monopolized by women. Women represented the intelligent and competent part of the community. In all probability the important discoveries of the first human culture can be attributed to women. Very likely it was woman who discovered the use of fire, invented cooking, clothing, sewing, and dressmaking. It is often assumed that women discovered and first engaged in agriculture. Man was in a subordinate position, a servant and assistant to feminine ingenuity. He was useful mainly as hunter and soldier. These professions may have implied dangers to which women should not be exposed. Woman was needed for the clever and finer work. Hunters and soldiers were not considered socially prominent.[12] From the matriarchal point of view we can understand why in Sparta male babies were

[11] All references to historical matriarchate, if not otherwise indicated, are taken from the vast material of scientific research compiled by Briffault (*The Mothers*) and Vaerting (*The Dominant Sex*). Cf. page 23.

[12] Many assume that the training and selection of man for physical strength became decisive in the development of man's social status. When human beings settled down and private property was established, the physical strength of man, not highly valued heretofore, became a vital factor in the protection and defense of that newly acquired property. The rather insignificant soldier advanced to the position of first power in the community, and there, until recently, he has remained. Sir Henry J. Maine (*Ancient Law*. J. Murray, London, 1906) considers the establishment of private property as the downfall of women. This change of settling down and establishing private property started a new phase of culture, called civilization.

27

killed immediately after birth when they were not very strong and healthy. They probably would not have made good soldiers; and they were otherwise of no use to the community. Not so girls. Their right to survive was never disputed, regardless of personal or physical deficiencies. They were accepted unconditionally as valuable members of the community.

In line with their social position went the sexual rights as the unquestionable prerogative of women. In Sparta, for instance, women had the exclusive rights of sexual liberties, while all restrictions, even extreme chastity, in sexual activities were imposed upon man. Under matriarchate, women choose their husbands, and the man has to wait passively. In some tribes, the female pays the family of the man she is going to marry, and removes him from his clan and instates him in her own.

WOMAN'S MODESTY A CULTURAL REQUIREMENT

These facts are evidence that the passive attitude of woman is not innate and is not based on her physical structure and her inherent function of motherhood. Her role as mother is not responsible for feminine passivity nor for her obligation to be pure and chaste. Neither are special sexual privileges a necessary consequence of man's capacity to procreate an unlimited number of children. The notion that modesty and morality are strictures upon only one sex has its origin in social conditions which produce certain conceptions of the "correct" sexual behavior. The following episode may illustrate the fact that sexual behavior depends merely upon social conventions.

28

It is said that Napoleon, when in Egypt, once walked through a little Arabian village. Entering a hut unexpectedly, he found himself confronted by several Arabian women. Immediately upon noticing the intruder, they excitedly lifted their skirts to cover their faces. To expose their genitals meant very little, but to show their faces to a man was unthinkable.

Evidently, then, social customs and traditions are responsible for modes of living which our generations, with their emphasis on natural science, like to trace to biological and physiological demands.[13] People living under matriarchate find as many good reasons for their habits as we do in our patriarchal society.

There are matriarchal communities where a woman who has had no lover has only a slim chance to marry. After having had many affairs she becomes more desirable. If no one has loved her before, something must be wrong with her. While in the masculine culture a woman with illegitimate children has less chance of finding a husband than a girl not so encumbered, under matriarchal conditions a girl who has proved her fertility before marriage is definitely preferred.

In our present culture, which until recently was strictly patriarchal, customs have differed from those under matriarchate where adultery was often forbidden only to man. For him, it could mean death. Our women have been expected to wait passively and innocently until a man should condescend to choose. Virginity was demanded of women, because any sexual experience before marriage was the privilege of man. It is hard to believe that until quite recently, however gifted or skillful or good-hearted and con-

[13] "Man is molded by customs, not by instincts." Ruth Benedict, *Patterns of Culture*. Houghton Mifflin Company, Boston, 1934.

29

siderate she was, nothing could help a girl if she had not preserved just one small membrane: her "honor." No man cared to marry her. Women who defied this social tradition became outcasts. There is little doubt that man, at the same time, had the social right to sexual license and unfaithfulness, in contrast to existing religious, moral, and even legal precepts. Men, indulging in sexual pleasures outside of wedlock, were hardly in danger of losing social status. Only recently has a change occurred. Today, this right of man is questioned but not yet fundamentally disputed, while twenty or fifty years ago the average man could enjoy his privileges without challenge.

THE DECLINE OF MAN'S SUPERIORITY

A radical change during the last hundred years is quite obvious. Masculine superiority is disappearing. The status of women is slowly but continually improving. Political rights of women already approach those of men. Women have new social and economic rights. They enjoy their own individual social status and practice almost every profession. It even happens that men become dependent upon their wives, socially or financially. Women take sexual liberties previously denied to them. How did all this happen?

Around the middle of the last century began the development of woman's rights as part of the social and economic transformation in the structure of our society. Just as the era of private property influenced the position of women and often ended matriarchal conditions, so again economic changes influenced the status of women. In the ascendancy of capitalism, each individual could acquire full civic rights and privileges by possessing the necessary amount of

30

money. The new social structure evaluated an individual in terms of dollars and cents. This led to an end of feudalism with its exclusive recognition of inherited nobility and to the establishment of human rights.

The ensuing liberalism gave every individual, at least theoretically, a fair chance to attain a socially accepted position. The idea of equal birthrights led to the liberation and emancipation of previously oppressed groups. Laborers, colored people, children, and women began to be regarded as human beings with their fundamental human rights acknowledged. Thereafter, man's power over woman decreased. In Europe, World War I accelerated this development. Replacing men, women gained access to professions formerly closed to them and earned new social recognition. With their new economic independence, they assumed new sexual freedom—a development hastened by the shortsighted conceit of man. For the new situation offered man a chance to satisfy his sexual desires with girls of his own social level without paying the price previously asked, namely, marriage. Now he could obtain a mistress who would demand neither payment nor surrender. He had neither to assume the full responsibility nor to give up his much coveted freedom. In suiting himself, however, he gave to his woman companion also the liberty of sexual expression and extramarital relationships. Thus his privileges began to evaporate.

LOVE AS WARFARE

At the time of humiliation and submission of women, the war between the sexes could be easily understood in terms of a revolt of the oppressed against their tyrants.

Terms of warfare are used in any language to describe love-relationships. They reflect this eternal warfare. An attractive person is "dangerous." First flirtations are compared to strategy. A woman is a fortress to be besieged and finally conquered by some male while she must try to "resist." Under assault she may "weaken"; and accepting her "enemy" completely is even called her "downfall." Even if these terms are used in jest, they show the spirit of warfare governing the love game. This fighting over the possession of one sex characterizes the union between the stronger— or the aggressor—and the weaker who has to be conquered.

One would imagine that when the oppression of one sex by another ceased the tension between them would lessen proportionately. However, quite the contrary is true. At a time when women had to obey, they had no choice and therefore accepted their status more or less as a matter of course. For instance, in former centuries it not uncommonly happened in some small villages in Germany that a hen-pecked husband received an ultimatum from his neighbors to the effect that if he was not willing or able to subjugate his wife, he must leave the village, together with his family. If one woman dominated her husband, the superiority of all the other men was endangered by her example. The man was always supposed to dominate. That was his right and his duty. Why? Because he wore the pants.

At the present time this strong and obligatory rule that man must dominate and woman must obey is fast becoming obsolete. In her new status, woman can rebel against oppression. She fights against a fate condemning her to submission. She demands rights, and is willing and able to struggle for them. Consequently, the relationship between

32

the sexes has become tenser than ever before; the war of the sexes has reached a state of violence which threatens to disrupt all cooperation and understanding between them.

THE PRESENT ANARCHY

This intensified warfare has led to a complete anarchy in the relationship between men and women. Until now, no woman or man could escape strict regulations. Now, with the fall of old laws, each man and woman has to establish an individual position in relationship to the other sex. No woman is obliged to submit herself, and no man can any longer rely on his mere maleness. As a result, we find today every couple revealing a varying distribution of power. Sometimes the man has all the authority, as in times of extreme masculine superiority, and in other cases a woman has the rights which her sex possessed under matriarchate. Every couple must find its own place at some point between these two extremes, and rarely do they succeed in establishing a true equilibrium. The old conviction that man is obliged to be superior is by no means abandoned. Many men and women still cling to this old tradition; though women often do not admit apprehension of being inferior, and men, while doubting their ability to dominate, still feel compelled to prove their superiority. The ensuing resentment of man and woman against the supposed masculine superiority was termed by Alfred Adler the "masculine protest." [14] Each regards the other sex as threatening the personal prestige; and, of course, general tension and hostility between the sexes increase.

[14] Alfred Adler, *The Neurotic Constitution*. Moffat, Yard & Company, New York, 1917.

As anarchy characterizes the relationship between men and women in any one country, so also there exists complete lack of regularity in regard to the position of women in the various countries. We can expect dissimilarities when comparing heterogeneous cultures, let us say the Oriental-Chinese with the European-American. But bewildering are the differences which are found among people belonging to the same circle of culture.

In each country, at the present phase of transition from patriarchy, every kind of relationship between a man and a woman can be found, ranging from complete domination by the man, to typical matriarchal control by the woman, co-existing with every shade of gradation between these two extremes. Everywhere the release of woman from submissive dependency progresses, though unevenly, reaching various stages in the different countries. Latin countries as a rule have lagged in this development. Emancipation started there later, perhaps because the process of industrialization was retarded. The status of women in Italy and in France, for example, can scarcely be compared with their status in Russia. Matriarchal conditions, however, do not exist in any country, although some men are inclined to regard conditions in the United States as matriarchal—by historical contrast. In reality there is no indication of matriarchal rule in the United States; it is only that American women have achieved a peculiar kind of equality.

THE STRUGGLE FOR AND AGAINST FEMININE EMANCIPATION

The development is swift. What can be said truthfully for one country today might not be correct a few years from now. A short and superficial analysis of the present situation in various countries may indicate the rapid changes. Strong patriarchal societies do not exist any more among cultured peoples. The last stronghold of masculine supremacy disappeared with the abolition of polygamy in Turkey and China. The change was not merely an administrative matter, but an expression of the alteration in women's position. China may perhaps still be considered slowest in regard to feminine emancipation. Except in the larger cities, men still may take concubines and not incur social disapprobation. They can even take a second wife without formality of divorce, provided the first wife has not borne a son. The social position of a woman is still enhanced by her having a son, although she is no longer completely worthless without one. In Chinese cities, women already participate in political, cultural, and gymnastic activities, something which always indicates social equality.

The situation in Germany is very interesting. World War I brought a definite and rapid trend toward equality, checked by the rise of National Socialism. For fascism revealed its reactionary character by its many feudalistic signs, often not recognized, and by its tendency to reinstate masculine hegemony. It reduced woman to her former place in the home and regarded as her main duty her function of breeder. It fostered some kind of polygamy by encouraging men to beget children freely. In reestablishing a slave society in some occupied countries, women "slaves" were used mainly as sexual objects and were even deported to houses of prostitution.

In Russia, the trend toward equality accelerated swiftly after the revolution. Women were granted more rights than they had been accorded anywhere else. But despite all legal equality, Russia still retained some signs of being a man's country. And the recent trend shows some definite reversion, expressed in the reinstated rules again giving the authorities the right to interfere and regulate the private sex life of the citizen. Early attempts to accept women as combatants in the army were later discouraged, and their place in the regular army is still disputed. Political power is still predominantly in the hands of men. This discrepancy between legal and factual equality is characteristic of the present conditions all over the world. An initial advance has been made in many countries by the establishment of constitutional equality, but practice lags.

Any frank discussion about the position of women in the United States is bound to meet with opposition. Our individual conceptions, based on tradition, cultural background, and education, dispose us to accept or reject certain facts and create emotions obstructing objective and causal analysis. Should we conclude that women actually have the same privileges as men, we would please many women. They would like to hear it, for they are proud of "their" achievements. Even some men would agree, either with a condescending smile, or with the complaint that women already have too many rights. Unfortunately for both of them, unbiased evaluation reveals facts which would irritate their complacency. Because—whether they like to hear it or not—women in America do not yet have full privileges. Anyone who wants to believe that equality is already established discloses thereby only his own patriarchal point of view, his fear that further progress would mean feminine supremacy. Women themselves add to the confusion. They bask in the glory of imaginary superiority, a delusion fostered by men who wish to divert women's attention from the real prize at stake. Let us face the facts: the four rights which we have defined, namely, political, social, economic, and sexual, are not yet equally accorded to women and men.

Politically: The Constitution concedes women the same rights as men. But, can women avail themselves of them? Full feminine suffrage is undisputed, but in practice women's eligibility to office is definitely limited. Even women can scarcely imagine a woman as a good president of the United States—although they reaffirm their belief in full equality. Men who for many reasons look up to women dispute emphatically their political acumen. (How wrong they are!)

Socially: It is in this field that American women have come closest to equality and, in some respects, may even appear to have transgressed it. But this superficial appearance is due to man's disdain of social "triviality." As a real test, a single man is still socially more acceptable than a lone woman. At a social function, extra women are as dreaded as extra men are desirable. A woman marrying beneath her social level risks more than a man in like case, and, most significant of all, women still accept the names of their husbands, and not vice versa.

Economically and professionally: Although statistics show that most of American property is owned by women —who manages the money? Definitely, men—who constitute the vast majority of financial executives. No one should be deceived by the fact that some women occupy high positions in business and commerce. They are still the exceptions; and as a rule feminine work is generally considered less valuable, as expressed in the lower wages that women receive for doing the same work as men. Few women who are so proud of their present status know that even today many universities either exclude their feminine faculty members from participation at university clubs or permit their entrance to the club rooms only through the rear door. Women are practically excluded from many professions, more *de facto* than *de jure*. Ask any woman physician about the many odds against which she has had to struggle. We rarely find women engineers, and the army and navy are still masculine prerogatives despite very recent inroads. Moreover, it is the general consensus that in times of widespread unemployment women should give up their jobs rather than have men remain idle. Whereas it is considered natural that men support their wives, a husband dependent financially upon his wife is regarded with contempt. Many marital problems have their origin in the conviction of men that masculinity is proved mainly through financial support. Women, successful in business, very often demonstrate overtly their tendency to behave "like a man," thereby demonstrating their doubt that they can be as good by being just a woman.

Sexually: All the sexual aggressiveness, for which American women are famous, cannot conceal the fact that, for the most part, women still wait for their man and not vice versa. Many tragedies in the love life of American women are caused by their desire to look up to the man whom they love. This spells tragedy, because it is very difficult for our well-educated and sophisticated girls to find a man who is superior to them, and when they do find him they resent his superiority and challenge it. Many girls refuse to go out with a boy shorter than they, although they like to look down on boys. Marriages in which the woman is her husband's senior are increasing in number, but still form a small minority. A woman is ashamed to admit that her husband is *not* superior, because it would mean he is not a "real man."

THE FALLACY OF GLAMOUR AND CHIVALRY

One fact that belies woman's assumption of sexual equality with men is the desire of the average woman to exhibit as much sexual attraction as possible. The glamour girl with the stream-lined body is admired, envied, and emulated as much as physical and financial facilities permit. Few stop to think that women in this manner voluntarily make themselves the *object* of men's sexual desire—not very differently from harem women. Display of sexual attractiveness has always been the method used by the inferior sex to gain the attention of the dominant sex.

Too little attention is paid to the difference between attracting attention and earning real esteem. Men pay womanhood the same price for humiliation as they have always paid before, and women today are as foolish in accepting the bribe. Moreover, the antique coins are still current. One venerable technique to which modern girls are susceptible is chivalry. It seems to be an expression of high esteem of womanhood. But is it really? Is not chivalry always an attitude of the strong and self-sufficient toward the weak and helpless? The same pattern of behavior toward a tower of strength would hardly be called chivalry. The chivalry which our men show might be interpreted by some women as the cowardice of a frightened male. But it is still the old masculine trick to bestow glory upon a woman in order to camouflage her real degradation. Chivalry was at its height in the Middle Ages. During the time of knights and minnesingers, women were the idol of the knight; service to his lady was his highest virtue. For her he fought his battles, in her name he won his victories. He wrote poetry in praise of her beauty, purity, and loveliness. So we are taught in schools, and the listening girls are enchanted by such high reverence of womanhood. They probably do not learn that when a knight wished to honor a guest exceptionally, he could bestow no greater compliment than offering him his wife for the night. She was the most precious and valuable gift he could lay at his guest's feet. No one realized the humiliation involved—nobody asked the lady her desire.

Chivalry always places women in inferior positions. If a girl expects her escort to open the door for her, she may believe that she is exacting consideration. She may even rationalize her dependency with her intention to make him feel useful. In reality, she places herself in the position of a helpless being who needs assistance and protection. Men's insistence on being of service sometimes expresses less consideration than girls like to believe. Helping women, treating them, bestowing gifts—these things are done much more for the donor's sake, as assertions of his superiority. Traditions developed under patriarchy invite men and women alike to continue the old hoax.

There are a few new techniques, but it is still the old game. Our present culture knows many ways of putting women on a pedestal which seem to offer reverence, but which only conceal contempt. Women are permitted to spend time and money for their beauty. They are given the opportunity to cultivate wit and refinement. They are free to visit museums, lectures, concerts and exhibitions, while men "have to" earn the money. Earning money seems to be the duty of men, but in reality it is their privilege. Instead of supporting women, they rule them. Many girls consider that men hold them in esteem in proportion to the money that men spend on them. They fail to realize that in requesting special consideration they request men to pay for what they buy: feminine company, beauty, smile, and make-up. The reason that men often marry beautiful and expensive girls is their desire to display them, just as they would display precious jewels; useless in themselves, these women only increase the prestige of the owner.

THE CULTURAL SIGNIFICANCE OF FEMININE EMANCIPATION

The increased self-assurance of women is bound to affect deeply our mode of life, as it has already done. It multiplies the difficulties which men and women find in living together. The general insecurity due to the present lack of economic, social, and political stability makes men and women more apprehensive of any threat to their prestige. The increased competition of women augments the suspicion of men; and man's attempt to keep woman within her limits embitters her. Each regards the other less as companion than as enemy. They live together, but they do not understand each other. They can't be without each other, but they can't get along with each other. Marriage no longer

41

offers even a solution of the sexual problem, just as divorce no longer solves the marital problem.

This conflict between men and women is only part of contemporary discord between human groups in general, such as the class struggle, the hostility between the generations, the fight between races and creeds, the war between countries and governmental systems. All this antagonism is based on mutual fear and distrust, originated by the attempt of those in power to govern and to maintain their dominance, and by the resentment and rebellion of millions of underprivileged beings who justly refuse to remain submissive. The end of the struggle cannot be expected until mankind has finished the process of establishing equality for all its members.

For the first time in human history we approach equality between men and women. We have not established equality yet, but the progress toward it is rapid. Love and sex were confusing for men throughout the ages because inequality never permitted a solid and stable equilibrium between the sexes. In certain cultures women were dominant, in others men. The dominance of one sex, when successfully challenged, turned into submissiveness. But equality never has existed. The present development characterizes the general trend in the social changes of our time. Although the approaching equality intensifies the struggle and the conflicts, the final outcome seems to be certain. Man is losing his supremacy, and woman will not be able to dominate again. Once a new and stable equilibrium between the sexes has been accomplished, a new harmony, unknown in past history, may be obtained. Then, probably, sex will stop being an eternal puzzle, which men wrote poems and dramas about instead of attempting to solve. Sex has been a threat to culture as long as men and women were living together as tyrants and servants. As the tool of unification of equals, it may take on forms unknown to mankind before. Thus the war between the sexes achieves significance for the whole transition period in which we live.

III.

THE CONCEPT OF SEX

THE SOCIAL FOUNDATION OF SEXUAL TRAITS

THE role that either sex has to play is, as we have seen, determined by the social structure of the surrounding community. The social conventions of today, however, exact no definite behavior from either sex. Each individual has to establish his own behavior pattern as man or woman. There are many ways of expressing "masculinity" and "femininity." It rests with each individual to decide what kind of man or woman he wishes to become.

As long as we regard masculinity as identical with superiority—and doubtless most men and women do so—the concepts that we develop of our own sexual role correspond to this superstition. Even the most ardent champions of feminine equality will probably aver that a "real man" is supposed to be strong, self-sufficient, courageous, and reliable, and that any man not meeting these demands probably shows "feminine" traits. The word effeminate—or, colloquially, sissy—indicates the general disparagement of "feminine" qualities. Actually, responsibility, the desire to

44

work, to contribute, and even to support, are not yet recognized as obligations of any human being, regardless of sex. The notion of man being the stronger sex is responsible for many odd ideas which confuse people's conceptions of their own sexual role, of their obligations or limitations.

Children at a very early age develop definite, but not always correct, conceptions of the social role attributed to their own sex. They are impressed and stimulated by the social implication of sex before they realize its emotional and physiological significance. As a rule, boys have much more liberty in every kind of activity. A girl who behaves like a boy is called a tomboy, a term implying specifically masculine traits. (The appellation tomboy, by the way, is far less contemptuous than the denunciatory term sissy.) Helping at home, cooking, cleaning, and mending are still demanded mostly of girls, especially in communities retaining European customs. Today, men wash dishes, too— sometimes; but still in condescension. Yet the practice indicates a general trend toward more cooperation, difficult for European men to follow.

Many girls believe that woman's place in society is subordinate. They either submit to their fate, seeking compensations in the feminine way, or they rebel and avoid anything feminine. The former attempt to win a respectable place in a masculine world by cultivating charm and helplessness and avoiding responsibility, in short, by striving for a typically "ladylike" deportment. The latter, those girls with strong masculine protests, refuse to achieve feminine maturity. They hate to look feminine; they abhor the menstrual function. Many girls do not go to this extreme. They may surrender to the general pressure and take pains with their appearance. But regardless of how feminine they may look, their protest becomes apparent on various occasions. They may try to prove that, as women, they can be as good as any man and perhaps even better. Very often they avoid recognizing their opposition to men and remain unaware of what has caused their sexual and marital difficulties.

A CASE OF TRANSVESTITISM

Rejection of the feminine role may reach almost unimaginable extremes. One day a young man consulted me. When asked about his problems, he revealed that he was a girl. The patient was in the middle twenties. The masculine appearance was caused not only by clothing, but by a definite way of speaking and by specifically masculine mannerisms. Even the voice was characteristic more of a man with glandular deficiency than of a woman. She had come because she needed help in a very unusual predicament. In order to get a job in Austria, it was necessary to present identification papers. Hers revealed her feminine name, which was embarrassing and confusing. She was now seeking permission to change her name to a masculine one. I was puzzled. How could she wear men's clothes since this practice was forbidden to a woman? She showed me a written permit from the police and explained how she had obtained it. When she wore women's attire, she attracted unpleasant attention in the street, because everyone believed she was a man masquerading as a woman. She walked like a boy, her whole attitude was decidedly mannish, so that the police were forced to give her this unusual permission.

A physical examination disclosed the normal primary and secondary sexual characteristics; the breasts were fully developed, the distribution of hair was typically feminine, as were the hips. The menstrual period was regular. A laboratory analysis proved that the gland functioned normally. There was not the slightest evidence of any physical or biological abnormality. Her unusual development proved to be caused by different factors.

She had been born in a rural district of Austria, the first child of a farmer. In that part of the world, girls were not in high esteem. Peasants need at least one boy to inherit the farm and to replace the father when he wishes to retire. Consequently, her parents had hoped for a boy. Unfortunately for the girl, a young brother was born two years later. It is not difficult to imagine her reaction to the situation. Realizing her precarious position, she refused to accept a secondary role. She made full use of the few years in her favor to maintain her superiority over her brother, physically and mentally. Yet it was not sufficient that he submitted to her dominance. He still was a boy and she only a girl. To win this battle, she had to overcome this handicap, too. So she tried to behave like a boy. She played with boys exclusively and became wilder than any of them. She was a regular tomboy, but even this compensation was insufficient. She delighted in dressing her brother in girl's clothes, while she herself put on his garments.

The parents enjoyed the masquerade and encouraged it. Everyone thought it was "cute." She heard many favorable comments about her looking like a boy; people remarked that she would have made a better boy than her brother, who had become quite subdued and docile, and, in his timidity, dependent upon his stronger sister. This success naturally encouraged her to continue and even intensify her efforts. When she grew older, she adapted herself more and more to this coveted masculine role. In every one of her movements, in her gait, in her mannerisms, she was a typical boy. She even became fond of girls, but in a protective and gallant way. When she began to develop physically, she fought against any sign of femininity. She hated her breasts. She pressed them down in tight garments so that they would be inconspicuous. She disregarded her menstrual function completely and did not let it interfere with any athletic activities. She never developed any feminine traits, skills, or features, and had her hair cut in boyish fashion.

The moment of her greatest triumph came when she obtained permission of the police to wear masculine attire. But the logic which she tried to defy brought her into new conflicts. Now she needed a masculine name. This was not easy under Austrian law; but as the authorities had been compelled to yield the first

47

time, it was necessary and logical to take the next step and grant her permission to use a name which was applicable to either sex. But a psychiatric recommendation was requested by the police. The girl was very enthusiastic. I tried in vain to convince her that, despite her successes, she was still fighting a lost battle. She still remained a woman, regardless of her ability to fool herself and others. Unless she accepted the role of her sex, she was bound to get into greater difficulties. But, like many people with sexual perversions, she did not want any advice or help and flatly refused to discuss her psychological problems.

To my surprise, she appeared again about one year later. I first thought she might now ask for psychiatric treatment. However, she came only to demand another service in her fight against society, which had marked her as an inferior being. She had fallen in love with a girl, and she expected me to make it possible for her to marry this girl. Of course, this was beyond anyone's power, and I never saw her again.

IMITATION OF THE "SUPERIOR" SEX

Whenever the established equilibrium between the sexes is shattered and the heretofore suppressed sex has the opportunity to rise, it imitates the behavior and mannerisms of the formerly superior sex. We have examples of this tendency in certain primitive communities. It may be during such a period of declining matriarchal structure that one peculiar form of behavior is observed—and often misunderstood and misinterpreted—namely, couvade. After the birth of a child, the father took the baby with him to bed and stayed there several days, while the mother had to perform all the household tasks and take care of father and child. It seems that the man tried to imitate the female role. Where women are dominant, everything typically feminine may appear desirable to men. One wonders whether men in that period would not have tried to bear children, too, had nature permitted.

Similar contemplations may explain the behavior of women today. In some levels of the population, smoking has become more popular among women than with men, and men have to resort to pipes in order to maintain some kind of distinction. The old American habit of women smoking pipes may have characterized social changes and an early emancipation of women during the time of American pioneering, which gave women tasks and rights they had never had before. There was more factual equality between men and women than in the old countries. The impulse, which may even counteract an initial dislike for smoking, stems from women's longing for masculinity, as it expresses in youngsters the desire to feel grown up. Other characteristic signs of our present state of transition are tendencies among women to assume masculine attire or hairdress. All these imitations do not signify actual equality, but indicate only an attempt by women to accentuate the change in their status.

THE FUNCTION OF THE SEXES

Each individual develops a certain conception of the role of his own sex, the acceptance or rejection of which modifies personal attitudes and affects almost every phase of everyday life. A woman's attitude toward domestic work, for instance, is a good test of what she conceives the role of women to be. The arguments pro and con must not deceive us. We can hear reasons why domestic work is desirable and why detestable—all equally good. The number of women who prefer housework to any other job is gradually diminishing. Many women resent this kind of "profession" because they consider it inferior or humiliating; they associate it with the derogatory conception of the feminine role. This association also keeps many men from participating in house duties. Housework has been the responsibility of women for so many centuries that it will take quite some time before men and women can look objectively upon certain duties necessary for the welfare of all.

During the period of their complete suppression women were to a certain degree excluded from artistic productivity. Actresses and dancers were socially degraded as indecent. Many women who look for their place in society now accentuate their interest in art, music, drama, dance, etc., to a point that art becomes almost a feminine prerogative. Is it not the privilege and duty of any human being, regardless of sex, to participate in artistic activity?

Many men have yielded to women their interest in the arts. A boy who is interested in studying the piano is often called a sissy. Women frequently find it difficult to induce their husbands to join them in reading books, in attending lectures or concerts, or in visiting museums and exhibitions. In fact, some women do not even try sincerely, because they are proud of this distinction between their respective interests. And men are only too delighted to pay this small price for the continuation of their supremacy.

The general concept of the masculine role seems to be that the man's job is primarily to make money. This conception is dangerous. It places exclusively in the hands of man the power which money still maintains. At the same time, it impedes man's appreciation of culture and general knowledge which could modify and temper his economic power. The danger of unscrupulous misuse of this power increases with the neglect of man's cultural development.

If women continue to be deluded by the advantages of convenient support, they will prolong their dependency.

The tendency to divide the social duties between the sexes is not based on biological factors, and specialized duties are fundamentally neither inferior nor superior. They are merely human obligations. In the distribution of work, certain tasks are allotted to each sex by custom and habit; they are considered as pleasant or distasteful according to the social position of the sex which performs each particular function. For the maintenance of marital life, the task of doing housework and that of earning money are of equal importance. If one earnestly believes in equality, one will be ready to do whatever is at the moment most necessary and most constructive and attach little importance to what is generally considered the proper sexual role. Despite all their nice words, few men or women are as yet ready to practice equality. The present problems of masculine and feminine adjustment cannot be solved merely by separating masculine and feminine activities and by establishing the respective competence of any sex in one well-defined field. Such a decision might relieve the competition temporarily, but it postpones the establishment of cooperation between equals.

SEX AND SOCIAL ORDER

The ability of men and women to regard each other as human beings and not as mere sexual objects is often thwarted by apparently unwelcomed sexual desire. Thus assailed, we are inclined to regard ourselves as the poor victims of untamed nature. Consequently, sex in itself seems a danger—a savage power threatening our culture and social relationships. It is not easy to realize that sexuality actually never arises against the interests of its so-called victim. The victim's intentions, indeed, are sometimes anti-social and often directed against the opposite sex. But sexuality itself is no threat; it is merely a tool.

But why are we always so apprehensive of sex—so easily irritated and disturbed by it? To young children sex causes no embarrassment. Is it just because they are unaware of it? And must free sex expression imply indecency? A careful observation of the sexual development and the establishment of the concept of sex in the child leads to an understanding of the mechanism of shame and sin, as does the sociological analysis of customs and habits in certain human societies.

Freud [1] believes that to maintain social life human society has to confine sex rigidly; that only by artificial suppression of certain sexual tendencies and of free sexual expression can social behavior be enforced upon human beings. Others regard the present laxity regarding sex as the cause of all evil: if people would become more "moral," the present social convulsions would cease. We know, however, of communities which, though strictly restrained, are nevertheless in a state of deep confusion and unrest, while other communities in which people live with candid, unconcealed sexual expression, even tolerating promiscuity, show little friction and maintain a highly organized social life. It is not sexuality which threatens society. The purpose of regimenting sex is not to save society; rather it is necessary in order to subdue one sex and deprive half of the members of

[1] Sigmund Freud, *Das Unbehagen in der Kultur*. Internationaler Psychoanalytischer Verlag, Wien, 1930.

society of their natural sexual rights. (See page 26.) Evidence to this effect appears in the fact that the dominant sex always manages to transgress the inconvenient restrictions. Modesty and chastity are imposed mainly on the subdued sex.

But this imposition puts some restrictions on both sexes, for women in their role of mothers instill their own shyness and timidity in their sons as well, and men must submit to certain restrictions because, to be acceptable, they must respect the feelings of wives, mothers, and sisters. The psychological consequences of the social restraints so imposed are the sense of shame and sin, which are instilled in the members of each society in order to maintain the social conventions characteristic of each community.

SEX AND RELIGION

Suppression and disparagement of sex are often ascribed to religious teaching. Religious creeds, however, represent merely the social conditions under which they were founded. We must recognize that religion in itself is not opposed to sexual licentiousness. Religious ceremonies involve extremely different attitudes toward sex acts, all the way from demanding them to forbidding them, according to the respective cults. On one side we find the religious prostitution of some ancient Greek communities, and on the other, the celibacy and chastity demanded by other religions. Christianity was established in a period when mankind first conceived the idea of equal human rights, without being able to materialize them in practice, owing to the political, economic, and social conditions which existed at that time. Society was not ripe for equality, and women were still definitely exploited. But, established for the first time, this ideal of equality between men and women demanded from man the same chastity which man had imposed upon women. Yet the church never could entirely prevent the dominant male from utilizing the privileges that society had bestowed upon him.

The present relaxation of strict moral demands, therefore, is not an attack on religion but on masculine superiority. The more liberal concepts relating to love, marriage, courtship, and divorce are neither anti-social nor anti-religious but the expression of the emancipation of women.

THE CHILD'S IMPRESSIONS OF THE OPPOSITE SEX

The individual's attitude toward his own sex corresponds to his attitude toward the other sex; both attitudes determine his behavior. The conception of the opposite sex is developed during early childhood. The first emotional responses to a person of the opposite sex are of lasting importance. Generally, father and mother set the first example of man and woman living together. A little child, with his limited comprehension, cannot recognize that the conditions at home are characteristic only of his own family and are not generally prevalent. For him the situation at home represents the whole world. And, therefore, the relationship between the parents appears as the only possible one between men and women. Thus the child constructs his conception of married life. Without realizing it, parents thus influence the child's attitude toward marriage. The parent of the opposite sex, as its representative, often affects the future sex-life of a child decisively. A sibling of the opposite sex may have the same fateful significance.

If a boy and his mother or a girl and her father are too devoted to each other, the relationship may become an obstacle to the child's later mating. A young boy who is favored and therefore very much spoiled and pampered by his mother cannot imagine that another woman will be equally devoted to him. Very frequently, this doubt prevents his falling in love and marrying. He is not prepared to meet a woman on the basis of give-and-take, as required in a happy marriage. The same often holds true in the relationship between father and daughter. A girl who is strongly attached to her father may expect from her husband the same understanding patience, guidance, and protection. She is apt to forget that no man of her own generation could possess the same relative superiority as her father, especially since girls now have for the most part the same educational and professional opportunities as boys.

This problem seems particularly prevalent in our day. Women protest against being the inferior sex, but, on the other hand, they dream of a husband to whom they can look up. They still cling to the idea that men must be stronger, more reliable than they. But how many men can a woman find to excel her as much as her father did when she was a child? She is bound to be disappointed, because she can rarely find such a man. Even should she eventually do so, she will not accept him. Resenting his superiority, she may withdraw from him or find fault so that again she may look down upon him.

CHILDREN BECOME AFRAID OF SEX

Our children grow up in a world of confusion, where all values, traditions, and customs totter. Their keenly observing eyes cannot fail to discern our fears and inhibitions. Their concept of sex is warped by the recognition of friction between men and women, and by the irritations caused by sex. The phantom of masculine superiority intimidates boys by imposing on them an obligation which they can never expect to fulfill, and invites girls to rebel against their secondary role. The masculine protest of boys and girls invests sex with all these threats of social humiliation, suppression, and degradation. The manner in which children make their first acquaintance with sex as a physiological mechanism intensifies the sense of danger. Long before children experience the functions of their own bodies, they hear about love-making, about sex relations and their consequences. What they hear is seldom pleasant. Adults talk freely in the presence of young children, because they believe that a child does not understand. Yet even if a child cannot understand the real meaning of words and ideas, he can sense the significance of remarks. So children learn about the dangers of pregnancies, about the disgrace connected with sexual experiences. Much of what they hear about sex is linked with suffering, disgrace, disadvantage, or even disaster. Especially girls become aware early that the disadvantages and dangers affect women mainly. No wonder that women are more inclined than men to regard sexuality as brutal, inhuman, and bestial.

SEXUAL ENLIGHTENMENT

This general impression of sex is fortified by the manner in which children are told about the "facts of life." The sexual enlightenment is very often accompanied by some psychic shock, because here a development otherwise most natural is generally impeded by the parents' reluctance to fulfill their natural obligations. Unfortunately, parents who were themselves brought up in restraint regarding sexual problems are embarrassed by the child's questions, and either do not answer at all, or, if they do not actually berate the child, avoid the issue. The child feels then that there must be something wrong with the object of his interest, if not with himself as well. Many conforming children, especially girls, never display any open interest in the subject, and their timidity and their tendency to avoid any contact with this "dangerous" problem may prevent their acceptance of any enlightenment, or produce a severe shock if they are forcibly confronted by the facts. Under more favorable conditions, children whose interest was originally frustrated go through a period of apparent latency, in which they show no interest in sex whatsoever, until the demand for more knowledge becomes more pressing. If they are very fortunate, they find teachers or other interested adults who provide the necessary information in a proper, casual, and clean manner. Generally, however, the sources of information are either the sordid ones offered by perverted adults, or pornographic literature, or the sensational and morbid discussions of half-informed school friends and playmates.

The whole problem could be so easily and adequately

handled if parents were willing and sufficiently trained. The two requisites for any adult questioned by a child are: (1) To be free of embarrassment and aversion. It is a natural right of the child to be informed, even at a very early age. Parents would not resent a child's asking where lightning comes from. But this question is far more remote from his vital problems than "Where do children come from?" (2) To answer every question the child may ask, correctly but never going beyond the demand made by the question. The phrasing of a child's questions expresses exactly the child's interest, and his ability to comprehend. Therefore, parents should listen carefully to the literal meaning of the question. The neglect of this rule is one of the most frequent sources of embarrassment for the parents. Instead of listening to the child's question, they imagine what he is going to ask next; but it doesn't happen, or at least it may not until months or years have elapsed. When the child first asks, "Where do children come from?" the literally correct answer is: "From the mother." There is nothing embarrassing in this fact except the unwelcome implications which adults only immediately associate with it. The child, however, is satisfied. Much later, he will ask: "How do children come into the mother?" The answer, again, is simple: "From the father"; and again it is without any too graphic implications, because a child is not interested in the physiological mechanisms. Even the question asked years later: "How do children come from the father into the mother?" can be answered with reference to love and marriage, which will satisfy the child's curiosity.

In that way, an understanding and emotionally adjusted parent can lead the child into maturity, when, for more technical information, the services of a teacher or a physician can be requested, if the great number of informative books do not satisfy the interest.

There is only one precaution required when a child asks questions. Parents must make sure that these questions are sincere expressions of interest, and not tools for gaining attention. Any person acquainted with educational techniques can easily recognize such counterfeit questions by their rapid sequence and their identical repetitious structure.

THE CHILD'S EARLY SEXUAL INVESTIGATION

Another factor impedes the development of a natural attitude toward sex in children, particularly in boys. Children, regarding their bodies as part of a strange world, examine themselves quite thoroughly. Over-anxious parents, discovering acts of self-investigation, become overly concerned and try, often clumsily, to prevent any touching of the genitals. It would be less dangerous to ignore these first investigations of the body than to frighten the child, for we know that early masturbation develops less from a natural inclination of the child than as a consequence of violent interference with harmless and insignificant actions. Most of the so-called bad habits in children are skillfully though unintentionally cultivated by parents and nurses who do not know that the normal child is inclined to repeat any movement from which he is forcibly restrained. Therefore, this interference of adults with curious investigation, far from preventing masturbation, simultaneously encourages the practice and instills mental conflicts which become far more dangerous during adolescence than any physical consequences. Implanting in the child a belief that sex organs are unclean and taboo and thus associating them with sin actually poisons the child's mind.

A child's first sexual experiences, also, affect his attitude toward sex. Such experiences occur very early. Growing older, he is likely to forget them, but all children do experience sexual excitement, some definitely and others only vaguely. Adults kiss a child on his mouth with no suspicion of his reaction. Titillations of a sexual nature are not restricted to any age. Some games, certain gymnastic practices or repeated movements arouse similar excitations. The sensation of fear may often provoke sexual stimulation. Children are unable to explain these feelings, although they derive great satisfaction from them. Parents could help mitigate harm from these mysterious experiences if they had the full confidence of their children. Most parents, however, through previous reprimanding interference, have lost their child's willingness to confide in them, as far as sex is concerned. Casual discussion without excitement or embarrassment can remove the child's bewilderment. A casual attitude prevents later conflicts and disappointments caused by established patterns of excitation.

How a childhood experience may considerably affect a later normal sexual adjustment was demonstrated by a woman who suffered from her inability to enjoy sexual intercourse. She longed for a specific gratification that she never could obtain in her marriage. In the course of our discussions, she became aware of what disturbed her. Once, as a little girl, while swinging she had experienced a peculiarly delightful sensation in her genitals. She could reproduce it by swinging. Later, although she expected the same excitement in a sexual relationship, she never found it. Consequently, she drifted from one man to another. Of course, this was not the real reason she could never find a suitable companion. This girl had an erroneous conception of love. She did not seek any real love, but was only seeking a particular genital excitement. Her first experience had given her an entirely wrong idea of sexual pleasure. Now she wanted only this specific pleasure and not a man's companionship. Obviously, what she expected to derive from a relationship and from marriage was in no way connected with love.

THE TRAINING FOR LOVE

Early experience of sex excitations, of infatuations, caresses, and passions are very important in our personal pattern of feeling and making love. Human love is very complex and intricate. Sex intercourse is only one part, and even this one portion is not simple and identical in all persons. We learn to love as we learn to walk and to talk, developing our own gait and our own dialect. The language of love-making is defined by early sexual excitations and molded by any new practice and experience. Our present behavior in love is trained and developed by all our previous experiences.

It is indeed unfortunate that the relationship between man and woman is obstructed by so many disturbing childhood experiences. The growing generation has little opportunity to develop an adequate impression of love. Rarely do they find it in their environment. Even ardently affectionate mothers very often have so many selfish, demanding, possessive qualities that it seems unwarranted to classify maternal love as an example of true love. The first impressions of sex and love are decisive, and too many of us grow up with the wrong expectations. "True Stories" and erotic movies are no compensation for unhappy marriages.

61

On the contrary, they distort reality and inflame the mind with pictures of sex attraction, beauty, and love-making which can never be attained in real life. How much disappointment and resentment is caused by these illusions of sex love! We seem to be caught in a terrible vicious circle. We ourselves are brought up with all kinds of mistaken notions and when we marry and rear our own children, we have little better to offer them.

Few parents are aware of how much their own attitude toward sex influences the ideas of their children. The child either accepts his parents' point of view or rebels and moves in the opposite direction. Surprisingly early in life, he develops a concept of love as a source of suffering or as an opportunity for mere pleasure and superficial gratification, or he learns that love and marriage provide the basis for human companionship. He can discover how much mutual help and stimulation can result from the cooperation of the sexes and can learn that love involves not only receiving but also, and primarily, giving.

ADOLESCENCE

The personal attitude of the growing child toward the sexes and toward his own sexual physiology determines the manner in which he later will approach love and marriage. It influences his choice of a mate and creates the particular conflicts which endanger or enhance his marital happiness. Any faultiness and distortion in this attitude becomes apparent during adolescence. This period of growing up is probably more troublesome today than in previous times. Parents tend to overprotect their children. They want to keep them dependent, partly because their own growing feeling of inadequacy makes them distrust the child's ability to take care of himself, and partly because their dire need for prestige does not permit them to loosen their cherished domination and become merely older but equal friends of their children. Consequently, they frown upon any expression of self-reliance or independence in the child.

The resulting friction between parents and adolescent children is particularly unfortunate for the child, because it coincides with a period of tension and apprehension caused by his physical development. Youngsters experience new feelings when their sexual glands mature. It is as if they were put into a new world. People long familiar suddenly provoke new and embarrassing feelings as the adolescent becomes aware of their sexual qualities. Boys and girls appear in a different light. Everything changes as the youngsters grow. They become awkward in their movements and feel insecure in the changing proportions of their limbs and bodies. No wonder they are extremely irritable and easily disturbed. The final conceptions of their own sex and their emotional and ideological attitude toward the other sex are established and stabilized in wavering and confused experimenting.

It is our duty to help these young people in their distress. They are entitled to our assistance during this most difficult period of their lives. At a time of perplexing changes in human relationships, friendship is a most important guide through all this confusion. Co-education helps to avert or at least mitigate the crisis. In acquiring a deeper understanding through mutual activity, the child may easily come to regard members of the other sex as human companions, and the sexual difference then becomes less important, and future compatibility is facilitated.

THE THREE FUNCTIONS OF SEX

We must recognize that human sex can be used for various purposes. First, it serves as a basis for procreation. Lust is the inducement of nature to lure every being into the service of maintaining and preserving the species. Religious and state laws regard this as the only permissible purpose of sex, any sexual activity outside of wedlock and any artificial prevention and interruption of pregnancy being prohibited or frowned on.

Second, sex can be used as a tool for personal gratification, mainly as a vehicle of pleasure. As man learned to escape nature's compulsion, he made sex independent of the process of procreation. Today, the two functions, namely fertilization and sex experience as pleasure, are for most people completely unrelated, the percentage of sexual acts which lead to pregnancy being rather small. But pleasure implies many sensations, some of which have completely different and sometimes contradictory meanings and significance. Pleasure can imply superficial and rather incidental gratification or deep emotions which involve the whole personality. The kind of gratification sought determines the role sex plays in the lives of different persons. There are those who consider pleasure of any kind as the only reason for living; to such persons, sex is merely an inexhaustible source—perhaps the only source—of enjoyment. Their hedonism or "pleasure hunger" as Wexberg [2] calls it, makes them grasp any opportunity for pleasure,

[2] Erwin Wexberg. Cf. p. 16.

with little or no regard to the price or consequences. Hedonists are usually disappointed and cynical people and, therefore, shortsighted in regard to life as a whole. They do not believe in their own future and happiness and, therefore, do not care what will happen later. For them, pleasure has to compensate for their feeling of being a failure. In the same category belong those who use sex for the purpose of gaining power, prestige, social status, or personal superiority.

Sex, however, can have a third function, that of unification. It is a tool which can unite two persons more closely than anything else. Through sex two may become one, physically and spiritually. This unifying function of sex also provides pleasure, of course. But it is a fundamentally different pleasure from the previously described pleasure. Its gratification is deeper and lasting. It implies giving oneself, while hedonism implies mainly taking advantage of another. While hedonistic excitement seeks variation and depends upon the spur of the moment, the desire for unification looks for stability and future happiness.

The subjective feeling of love may employ all three types of sexual functions. The first and the third, however, involve a long-range program, while the second, the tendency to seek mere gratification, is likely to neglect human and social values.

It seems that in our time sex has lost to a great extent its first, primary function, but people have not yet found the third, the fulfillment of unification. The concept of sex as being useful only for pleasure is prevalent and deprives people of deeper gratification, of lasting love, faithfulness, and devotion.

IV.

CHOOSING A MATE

How we choose a mate is a decisive test of our concept of love and marriage. At the moment of choosing, we put into operation all that we have thought, expected, and feared. The choice of a wrong partner can be regarded as the first step toward marital discord, or as the last step in a misguided approach toward the other sex. Many people make no step at all. To choose or not to choose—that is the question which plagues them eternally.

The act of choosing is not only highly important, but also extremely significant, psychologically and scientifically. Like a flash of lightning, it suddenly illuminates the whole situation and sheds its glaring light on the forces which produced the bolt. But the analogy of lightning explains even more about the process of choosing.

INTERPERSONAL COMMUNICATION WITHOUT AWARENESS

The moment we decide in favor of someone, we conclude a number of interactions which preceded this final step from both sides. In one instant, two persons who meet for

66

the first time can communicate to each other untold impressions, opinions, and promises, and come to an understanding without either of them becoming aware of his participation in the game. They talk with their eyes, expressing admiration, suspicion, disdain. Little movements of the hands, facial gestures, unimportant words, the tone of the voice, the gait, and the whole appearance reveal the entire personality and its reaction to the other one. Whatever goes on between two human beings is reciprocal and promoted by both, although it may look as if one of them started the motion and hence is responsible for the action. Such a conclusion, however, is a mistake based on inadequacy of observation. Our inaccurate eyes misinterpret the lightning bolt as striking from one direction alone, although we know today that it is a rapid consequence of discharges of electricity from both poles simultaneously.

We know more about each other than we realize. Our conscious impressions are but a small part of our actual knowledge which is based on what we used to call intuition, premonition, or, less flamboyantly, a hunch. An analogy with the eye may clarify this mechanism: Only a small central part of the retina (the tissue of the eye which enables vision) permits sharp distinction of shape and color, while the larger multifold surrounding section of the retina serves to give vague impressions of the location and the movement of objects. Therefore, the picture which we encompass with our sight is much wider, richer, and deeper than that which we can focus by sharp attention. This is true of other senses as well. With the ear we recognize one tone without being aware that its qualities are derived from overtones which we cannot directly perceive. This example is necessary to understand that acceptance or rejection of another person is based on much knowledge and agreement which entirely escapes our own conscious observation. Without realizing these psychological mechanisms in the process of mating, we cannot comprehend the essential problems involved.

MATING SERVES SECRET PERSONAL ANTICIPATIONS

The secret aims and expectations of a person guide him like a compass. Involuntarily, he responds only to those stimulations which fit into his plans and recognizes only those opportunities that confirm his expectations. A girl who wants to get married invariably chooses a man who provides her with what she demands. Her demands, however, are not necessarily limited to the common-sense requirements which the average American girl is taught to exact from her future husband. Although the conscious expression of these marital desires may vary—one girl looking for companionship, another for social and financial betterment or security, the third for fun and excitement—they all want cooperation, understanding, consideration, devotion, and faithfulness. Very few of them, however, choose a husband at all capable of maintaining those qualities.

And yet the selection is never fortuitous. There are deep personal demands which influence the final decision; and, unbelievable as it may sound, everyone gets from his mate just the treatment that he unconsciously expected in the beginning. The demands which are gratified when we suddenly or gradually accept one person as our right mate are not conventional—not those of common sense. We feel

68

attracted when we have met somebody who offers us through his personality an opportunity to realize our personal pattern, who responds to our outlook and conceptions of life, who permits us to continue or to revive plans which we have carried since childhood. We even play a very important part in evoking and stimulating in the other person precisely the behavior which we expect and need. In other company the same partner might behave altogether differently.

THE PAST INFLUENCES THE PRESENT

One factor which often influences the selection of a certain person is his resemblance to other persons previously objects of our affection. The resemblance may lie in physical features or mannerisms or, what is more important, in character traits which promise the re-establishment of an already familiar relationship. Previous experiences with a person of the other sex influence our attitude in the first meeting with any new acquaintance. The more intense these earlier experiences were, the deeper their influence in regard to the establishment of new relationships. The strength of these early impressions can be measured not only by the intensity and duration of the emotions previously aroused, whether pleasant or disturbing, but by the influence they have had on our outlook on life. This fact explains why early childhood experiences, even if they were of a rather casual nature and not connected with strong emotions, so frequently affect the choice of a mate. They played an important part in the establishment of our life plan which later relationships can scarcely change. A man who was a pampered child and relied upon the help of others will

69

probably throughout his life be especially impressed by women who accept him as such. The more intensely he was pampered, the earlier it happened and the longer it lasted, the more closely will his later choices resemble the woman who pampered him—generally a mother or older sister. Such early impressions lead often to a definite taste in regard to the opposite sex.

INDIVIDUAL TASTE

Our present taste in love can often be traced back to persons of the other sex who in the past responded to our desires. Our present attitude may be aggressive or retiring, courageous or timid, and may even change from time to time. At any given moment we rely on those past images in making our choice, in accordance with our personal needs and the requirements of our life situation.

Our predilections, however, also reflect our thoughts and phantasies, which are not only based on personal experiences, but stimulated by our whole environment. Personal taste expresses not merely the desire of a single individual, but the evaluations of the group to which he belongs. The mate felt to be ideal and most desirable follows a pattern of ideal figures created by the imagination of the whole group. Ideals change as social conditions change. Fashions, the style of women's clothes, and even their figures, are influenced by social conditions and the status of women, as by all events which influence the life of society. War, prosperity, depression are immediately reflected in styles of dress; it is astonishing how quickly and precisely slight changes in the social position of women are registered in fashions. Hairdress, length of skirt, accentuation or disguis-

70

ing of contour and figure are characteristically responsive, as woman, by rendering her appearance more masculine or feminine, not only changes man's taste but expresses her evaluation of man's opinion.[1] The great popularity of a given artist and his success in influencing the erotic taste of innumerable people shows that this artist senses the general social trends and becomes their exponent, often without realizing it. Movie stars and actors in general have an eminent place in representing general desires and influencing the formulation of ideal types. It is hardly possible to distinguish the contribution of a powerful personality from the public demand. Influence and response are probably interdependent.

A new and puzzling contemporary development, namely, a definite tendency to choose an older man or woman as a mate, seems to require some consideration and analysis. First, men today have been pampered children more frequently than in the past. Second, the lowered status of men makes them more likely to refuse the highly responsible position of the superior male and to look instead for a mother.

On the other hand, the girl who still has a longing—her cultural inheritance of the past—for such a superior man, once found him in the person of her father, but does not encounter him any longer among the men of her own age. She often looks for an older more experienced and better established mate who offers fatherly consideration and

[1] A chaotic combination of feminine and masculine features is characteristic of American fashions; our society combines a strange simultaneous mixture of feminine emancipation and suppression, rarely found anywhere else. The feminine fashion either imitates masculine patterns or accentuates extreme femininity by daring aggressiveness through exposure.

71

protection, not to be found among the more competitive contemporaries. Older persons, on their part, are more willing to accept responsibility in exchange for the gratification of their superiority over admiring juniors; their greater experience makes it easier for them to maintain their superiority without antagonizing their partners. The choice of a much older or younger partner may represent a constructive tendency toward a happy union or a striving after cheap success; all depends upon whether it is the expression of courage or of timidity.

THE SIGNIFICANCE OF BEAUTY

Closely related to taste is the significance of beauty. Artists may look for a *sectio aurea* to decide objectively what is beautiful, but the average person still judges beauty quite subjectively. Beauty is what we like—whatever we enjoy seeing. Personal taste arbitrates beauty, particularly in regard to sex. Feminine beauty, masculine strength—for strength in a man passes for beauty—these are decisive factors in the choice of a mate. But why have we chosen these particular standards? Old theories suggest that these two attributes indicate health, and as health is of primary importance in procreation, they would seem to provide a sound foundation for marital selection. These theories, however, do not explain why we have made beauty a feminine prerogative, while strength is the criterion in a man.

That these are our standards is evidence of our patriarchal thinking. Actually, health is not the basis for the esteem in which beauty and strength are held; types of morbid beauty are not less attractive erotically and muscles often hide decayed bodies and deteriorated minds. The truth is that in a patriarchal society beauty and strength are social values; the female sex must be the "fair" one because it trades on its appearance, catching the eye of the selecting male, who afterward, proudly demonstrating his wife's beauty, can boast of his conquest and excite the envy of other males. He, on his side, has impressed his partner with his conquering strength, which guarantees protection and domination. A pretty man looks effeminate, because he operates with feminine methods, while a muscular woman looks masculine. Beauty and strength thus became the basic elements of sexual attraction, now called "sex appeal." Current social changes in the relationship between the sexes will modify these values, too. Feminine beauty may cease to be a social asset and be judged on the basis of a more individual private preference, or may even become utterly insignificant.

The implications of the term sex appeal exemplify such changes. Although seemingly physical in nature, sex appeal becomes increasingly an expression more of mental and emotional processes than of physical qualities. This becomes more apparent as the attraction of mere beauty diminishes. But what distinguishes sex appeal from beauty? Beauty evokes admiration in men, sex appeal excitement. The girl with sex appeal intends to excite, whether she is aware of this tendency or not. And furthermore, she knows she can succeed. Lack of physical appeal is no obstacle, as beauty is only incidentally an asset. Every woman can develop sex appeal if she becomes interested in erotic conquest and discovers her ability to excite. Many plain women suddenly become attractive in response to unexpected attention and affection, which change their conception of themselves. Sex appeal in men does not need "war paint and disclosure of hidden allure to attract the excited imagination of females, but it expresses the same will to conquer and the confidence of success, as do feminine charms.

Despite the high esteem in which sex appeal is held, it is still foolish to be impressed by it. Persons with sex appeal generally do not make good mates. When a girl with sex appeal marries, she either retains her desire to excite men and makes her husband jealous and unhappy, or if she finds satisfaction she loses her sex appeal and with it her husband, who chose her for this reason. In either case, she shifts the equilibrium which existed at the time of her marriage. The desire to excite indicates a thirst for gratification which can never be quenched. It is directed rather toward attention and new conquests than toward contentment and lasting companionship.

Beauty, by stimulating such aberrations, can likewise become a handicap rather than an advantage to marital success. Beautiful girls may rely more on the attention they can expect than on their ability to play a constructive part in society. False ambition and vanity, combined with dependency upon the opinions of others, create a lack of self-confidence. Thus beauty, which evokes pampering, too frequently hinders the development of constructive qualities and impairs the sense of cooperation. Hence, many beautiful women cannot succeed in their marriages. They receive attention and admiration; they find pleasure in erotic gratification; but their lives often remain empty. The threat of old age hangs over their heads. The glamour girl and the Don Juan are only two of many types of unsuitable mates. Nevertheless, these types are often chosen.

Tastes and predilections are conscious inducements for falling in love with a given partner. They express, however, inner motivations of which nobody is fully aware. The whole process of selecting and choosing is based upon deeper psychological processes, which are not accessible to introspection and self-analysis. While everybody knows and feels what he wants, recognizing his desires and wishes, he remains unaware of his real goals, aims, and purposes, especially when his intentions are not in line with common sense and are directed against social conventions and the logical demands of a given life situation.

A socially well-adjusted person with courage, self-confidence, and faith in his own future and happiness will intuitively choose a partner who promises happiness and harmonious union. A discouraged, pessimistic individual may still desire love, affection, and marriage, but his pessimistic expectations will lead him astray. He either will not recognize a good chance or will run away from it, as it does not fit into his scheme of action. His inner defensiveness may induce him to develop a variety of attitudes and actions which provoke and, at the same time, excuse sexual and marital difficulties and frustration.

THE CREATION OF DISTANCE

"Distance" is a characteristic weapon of defense. Anyone avoiding complete self-surrender may create distance in various ways. One is by the division of love objects. Being attracted in different ways by several persons of the other sex makes it impossible to accept any one person entirely. The distinction between spiritual love and sexual attraction, between affection and sensuality, proves effective for this purpose. A man may love an exalted, refined woman whom he does not dare approach sexually; she may, it is true, conform to his image of mother or sister as Freud [2] suggests, but this psychological "revelation" misses the point. This type of woman has very likely been deliberately chosen by the man for the purpose of maintaining distance, often enough to the dislike of the girl concerned, who is not at all pleased by such veneration. The image which one uses, and the purpose in using it, must be distinguished one from the other. We misunderstand the situation if we content ourselves with discovering an incompletely over-come "incestuous fixation" on mother or sister. Likewise, exclusive preference for socially or mentally inferior women as objects of sexual gratification has little to do with avoiding a venerated "mother image," but more with the preser-vation of masculine superiority and the prevention of a satisfactory union in marriage. "Devaluation as well as idealization creates distance." (Alfred Adler) [3] If we feel sexually attracted to a person whom we cannot esteem personally while another person induces confidence and admiration but does not stimulate us erotically, it is not the fault of the other person. In reality, we merely offer our-selves in installments. We accept one only sexually and the other one only spiritually—and blame the other one for not having aroused us in both ways. What a trick in confound-ing cause and effect!

[2] Sigmund Freud, *Über einen besonderen Typus der Objektwahl beim Manne, Sammlung kleiner Schriften zur Neurosenlehre.* Internationaler Psychoanalytischer Verlag, Wien, 1922.
[3] Alfred Adler, *Das Problem der Homosexualität, Erotisches Training und erotischer Rückzug.* S. Hirzel, Leipzig, 1930.

CHOOSING AN INELIGIBLE PARTNER

Another familiar and common way to gain distance and avoid complete union is the choice of a partner who is already bound by other ties. This is a very successful manner of shunning responsibilities. Many men and women have an unfailing instinct for partners who are no longer free. They themselves are puzzled by their "bad luck" and wonder why each one to whom they feel attracted turns out to belong to someone else.

A young girl complained about this kind of misfortune. She never succeeded in disentangling her choice from previous ties. "Really never?" she was asked. She admitted, "Yes, once." But under what circumstances! She was deeply in love with a man whom she greatly idealized. Suddenly her feelings for him vanished. She had thought, up to this very moment, that the reason she fell out of love was that she had become aware of his shortcomings and discovered that she had previously put him on a pedestal which he did not merit. What she had been unable to realize before was that this change of attitude occurred just when the man had finally broken off relations with a former girl friend and decided to turn completely to this girl. Such occurrences are not coincidental. Now she was on the spot and had to live up to her ardently avowed devotion. This was the real cause of her change of mind.

This story demonstrates a very important point. A person with a psychologically correct attitude diverts his interest in a prospective mate when he realizes that there are insurmountable obstacles. To a person who avoids union, however, this is the proper occasion for falling in love. He gives himself the "green light." On the other hand, he loses his interest when circumstances unexpectedly become favorable. Then he puts on the red light.

77

THE GREEN LIGHT FOR THE WRONG DIRECTION

A man had tried, until the age of forty, to get married. He tried hard, but unsuccessfully. When he was around twenty, he had wanted to marry a girl who hesitated to marry him. He had stunned her by proposing as soon as they met. His proposals continued, but the more he urged, the more she hesitated. The more she withdrew, the more he rushed her. Finally he gave up. Years later, he found out that he had dropped her just at the moment when she was earnestly considering marrying him. Merely a coincidence? He then fell in love with a woman who was married. For years he tried vainly to induce her to leave her husband. She showed no inclination, and he gave up.

He could not find anyone else for some time, until he fell in love with a widow. They went together steadily for many years, but she also refused to marry him, although she admitted that she loved him. But she preferred to retain the pension of her late husband, which gave her complete independence. He could remember clearly the day when he first realized that he was in love with her. On a Sunday afternoon one summer, they sat together in the garden of a restaurant, and he told her that he would like to take her to the country some day to visit his parents. She hesitated, and then said, "No." He felt a sudden pain and was brought by this shock to realize how much he cared for her.

What he did not realize is that at this moment he became aware of her disinclination to marry him, which was expressed in her refusal to meet his parents. This was the green light for him —a sign that there was no hope, a condition which would indicate a red light for anyone else. When he had finally left her and came to consult a psychiatrist, he was desperate, although still looking frantically for a wife. It was difficult to imagine how he could ever find one, because he had established a clever scheme of objections, which he applied to every new prospect introduced to him by well-meaning friends and relatives. If the woman was close to his age, she did not attract his desire, and if the girl was young, he feared he could not satisfy her and that she would betray him. The suspicion of being cheated and

78

married only for his money and financial security was aroused by a poor girl, and a girl with money or income frightened him by her independence, which deprived him of influence.

An analysis disclosed the following history. He had been reared in the Austrian countryside, where men enjoy distinct preference. He was deeply impressed by the superior role which his strong and dominant father played in the family; he tried his best to imitate his father. His mother and his sister were the victims of the tyranny whereby the boy tried to assert his masculinity, or, rather, his conception of masculinity. He wanted to hold the same position as his father, but doubted his ability ever to be as strong as his father seemed to be. That was his tragic conflict. He became hesitant and over cautious on one side— and over aggressive on the other. He wanted to marry and become the "boss," but, at the same time, he feared his incompetence. Without realizing it, he committed himself to others only if, and as long as, they did not want to marry him. Thus he retained his eagerness to marry, while preserving his solitude.

During psychotherapy, the patient began to understand himself. He lost his tension and the nervous symptoms accompanying it. Some months after treatment, he came to tell me that he was engaged. I was interested in finding out how he, who always asked how and where to find a suitable girl, had finally managed to meet one. He told me the following story.

While attending a circus, he discovered, way down in the first row, a good-looking young girl, who attracted him considerably. While considering how to approach her, he noticed that she was accompanied by a young man who looked vaguely familiar. So he took a chance and went to meet them and actually had more luck than he had expected. Upon introducing himself to the man, he found that they had met on a trip—and that this man was "only" the girl's brother. A few weeks later, he and the girl were engaged.

This story is significant, because it illustrates the problem. When people ask, "How can I find a mate?" shall we tell them, "Go to the circus?" Life offers plenty of opportunities to all of us, but it remains for us to make proper use of them. Only wrong attitudes and expectations are responsible if we find either no one at all or meet only the wrong people.

79

THE APPEAL OF DEFICIENCIES

A great many people fall in love with or feel attracted to a person who offers the least possibility of harmonious union. Very often good marital prospects are neglected in favor of a very questionable choice. Two secret tendencies are chiefly responsible for this: the desire to maintain one's superiority, and the hope of suffering. The one induces the selection of an inferior or inadequate mate; the other the choice of someone who, despite certain qualities, brings dissatisfaction or even torture, granting only the solace of martyrdom. Very often a partner is chosen for his faults. It is rather easy to discover why persons united in a miserable marriage have chosen each other. The complaints which anyone voices against his mate indicate exactly the qualities which stimulated attraction and love before marriage.

A woman was living in an exceptionally unhappy marriage. Her husband gambled, never had a steady job, took her money by force, if necessary, lied, and was utterly irresponsible. She was a fine, sincere, and good-natured woman and did not understand why she, of all people, had to have such a mate—she who had always pined for a quiet home and a decent husband. She admitted, however, upon questioning, that at the time when she met her husband, another man had proposed to her. According to her description, he was the type of man who would have given her security and comfort, companionship and devotion. But she preferred her husband, who was even then a good-for-nothing, gambling and chasing after women. She felt more attracted to him, without knowing why; she thought he needed her, that she would be able to reform him and bring out the good qualities which she sensed in him. These were her rationalizations; the real reasons she did not know. As a child, she had been neglected in favor of her brothers, and, feeling inferior to them in one sense—her sex—had tried to make herself superior in other directions, by working harder than her brothers, being

80

more reliable, assuming responsibilities beyond her obligations. As a grown woman she still needed this sense of superiority— hence her choice of a weak and unstable husband.

Frequently a person remains in the memory as an ideal mate—the one lost chance of a lifetime. Why do we recognize such suitability only after the occasion is lost?

A patient told me that he had fallen in love with a girl who was so fine and congenial that he never hoped to find her equal again. She would have been an ideal wife. He cannot understand why he always, by hook or crook, managed to stir up quarrels with her. Although she was fond of him and he liked her very much, the association broke up because of these incessant quarrels. He admits now that, during their courtship, he had often thought that she was too intelligent and efficient for him, and that he would never be able to live up to her level. Shortly afterward, he fell in love with an insignificant, spoiled, and flighty girl who, however, offered him a chance to prove his own superiority. He married this girl; and, of course, his life with her was miserable.

Another patient complains about his wife, because she has no initiative, no efficiency. She is too passive and takes no responsibility. The patient asserts that he would have been a success, despite his nervous condition, if his wife were only more capable and self-reliant. As it is, he has to take care of everything himself, in and out of the house. She is more hindrance than help, cannot economize nor make a pleasant home. Why in the world, then, did he marry just her? He says he didn't know then what she was like. I invited her for a talk. She is a shy person, but sincere and frank. Her story is that he curbs her activity and removes every opportunity to be useful. Before she has even started to act he has discouraged her and taken the task upon himself. She has observed that he gets angry and irritable if she assumes any initiative or responsibility. In order to avoid friction she must leave everything to him. She believes that he wants her to be dependent on him, and she is probably right.

This explains why he married her: he fell in love with her

81

precisely *because* she was inefficient and passive. This is what he wanted—an inferior person who would look up to him. If she were different, his domestic superiority would be endangered; moreover, he would have no excuse and no scape-goat for his shortcomings in the world at large. He was an oldest son who wanted to remain first. Within his family he had his status, but he found it difficult to realize his ambition outside his family.

A man complains about a domineering wife who grants him only a small allowance, never leaves him alone, and nags and criticizes him. It is most probable that he married her just for these qualities. A pampered mother's boy, he was shy in contact with girls. When he first met this one, he was delighted with her solicitude. She made suggestions about his clothes and conduct. Instead of being taken out to expensive places, she preferred quiet evenings at home, in order to save money. She was quite different from the other girls he had met, and he liked it. When they married, he did not like what he himself had provoked. Didn't he really know what she was like? Or had she changed? Not at all. But he probably would have been no happier with any other wife, had he chosen another.

Very often, disappointments with one type of mate lead to remarriage with the opposite type. Some persons with a rather rigid pattern of life select the same type over again, and never learn to get along. More courageous ones choose the opposite extreme, which, however, does not prove conducive to marital happiness. A woman who had been deeply disappointed by an unscrupulous, inconsiderate husband, fell in love, after her divorce, with a very methodical and dependable man who was so cautious that he never married her. A man who had been dominated by his first wife afterward married a little flighty girl who had no sense for marriage, housekeeping, or children. The extremes have the same effect—disunity and friction instead of cooperation.

However sincere the complaint, a change on the part of

sband or wife in the direction of greater conformity would not help. Disturbing qualities not only attract, but are constantly provoked anew during marriage. Even when former virtues turn into faults, these faults serve to maintain the once established equilibrium. Thrift in a fiancé is seen as miserliness in a husband; generosity as extravagance; assurance, lust for domination; orderliness turns into exaggerated meticulousness; fondness for home life becomes dull domesticity. But it would be dangerous nonetheless for the criticized persons to alter their behavior. The patient who complains so bitterly of the inability and inefficiency of his wife resents any sign of self-reliance in her. The henpecked husband would feel neglected without "due" consideration. The woman who pays the debts of a gambler husband would miss the satisfaction of her responsibility and self-sacrificing goodness if her husband became orderly and "dull." The husband who complains about his wife's flirtatiousness would probably lose interest in her if she stopped attracting the admiration and attention of other men. Everyone is deeply interested in maintaining the faults of his partner.

THE LIFE STYLES RESPOND

The factors which lead to the choice of a partner are correlated with the conflicts which later result during the marriage. The relationship is not merely one of conscious choice and logical conclusions; it is based more profoundly upon the integration of the two personalities. At the instant when two persons decide to marry, they sense the congruity of each other's life styles. Even a marriage contracted as a thoughtless incident of drunkenness and sexual excitement represents a deeper agreement of two personalities than is generally credited. Although such a choice is considered purely accidental and generally leads to disappointment and quick dissolution, it is a true reflection of the two personalities involved. Their general directions in life have merged, regardless of how long their agreement lasted.

Agreement between two persons and congruity of their two life styles do not mean identity of the life styles. On the contrary, they demand complementary differences. Two individuals each of whom wants to be dominant hardly fit together. Neither would two martyrs. The distinction must be made, however, between psychologically insignificant qualities and the all-important life style. Husband and wife may both be ambitious or both resentful and yet may get along; their identical qualities may unite them more closely. But the decisive point is neither the qualities nor, we may add, the common interests, as many believe, but actually the basic pattern of life, the method by which they strive for superiority or suffering, for success or security. This explains why so often an oldest child marries a youngest one; a dominant individual a submissive one; why the brute finds a saint, and the rogue his protective victim. These types, paired as shown, constitute in varying degree the average married couple. And the extremes are not so exceptional as one might believe.

Mrs. F. developed her personality in competition with a younger sister, whom she surpassed mentally, scholastically, and socially. She maintained her own position as the first one by pushing her rival down and thereby gaining the approval of the parents. Without knowing it, she thereby contributed to the utter deficiency of her sister. She married a man who grew up in the shadow of an over-ambitious older sister. Despite the constant quarrels and profound misery of their marriage, despite their mutual complaints about their "incompatibility," they fitted perfectly into each other's life. Although the wife found her husband's lack of intellectual interest and social graceless-ness unbearable, it was obvious that she gained by it—and prob-ably got what she had looked for.

Mrs. O. grew up as an only girl among several brothers. She had a strong masculine protest and always wanted to play the role of a man. Her husband, on the other hand, had an older brother of very masculine tendencies. He developed early the idea that he was not a "real man." While he ran away from any masculine competition and found his refuge in art, his wife fought his battles with the masculine world, not without blam-ing his lack of strength and effeminate nature for their mutual dissatisfaction and social, as well as financial, difficulties. They were constantly at odds with each other, although they certainly fitted together.

The following marital history may sound fantastic, and yet it concerns a couple regarded by their friends and associates as an ordinary middle-class family. Both husband and wife are highly intelligent and keep their secrets well. The girl had married her mother's lover. Why did she fall in love with him? She hated her mother, partly, it is true, because she resented the mother's infidelity and her disrespect for the father, but chiefly because her mother ostensibly preferred a younger sister. Since child-hood, she had felt rejected and neglected in favor of her sister and had sought compensation in merely sensuous gratification of various kinds. Although she professed high regard and ad-miration for her husband, she probably recognized the exact caliber of this man who "seduced" the daughter of his mistress. She could have suspected what was in store for her when she used every possible means to make him marry her.

Immediately after their wedding, he expressed strong resent-ment toward her, told her bluntly that he did not care for her; he felt she had tricked him into marriage. She accepted this attitude quietly, kept her love burning, and waited for his re-turn when he left her shortly afterward. Sure enough, he came back—because they fitted together. But he brought her a gift: gonorrhea. Even that did not disturb her love for him. Then he left her a second time, shortly after she had borne him a child. She still waited patiently until he returned again—this time with syphilis. Even that was no reason for her to leave him. The few persons who knew the situation could not understand her patient submission. Some tried to explain it on the basis of sexual bondage. Of course, sensuousness was her only ideal and she was willing to suffer for it. But, at the same time, she used her suffering as a means to punish her husband, as previously she had punished her mother with the same trick. She thereby gained superiority over her guilty torturer. Many little incidents revealed how she provoked mistreatment from her husband, when a little use of common sense could easily have put him in his place. Her secret intention to be the "innocent" victim was the reason why she selected this man as a husband, and why she clung to him time and again after he had brutally mistreated her. Actually, in this marriage the cardinal problem was not the husband as one might think, but the "saintly" wife.

THE REAL REASONS FOR ATTRACTION

The real reasons why we choose a mate usually remain secret and are supplanted by plausible rationalizations. Many believe in marrying for security. There is no security obtainable through marriage. There is no security in life at all. Marriage does not solve any problem; it remains a problem in itself, which has to be solved, and merely adds a new task to the others with which life confronts us. Some marry for social or financial improvement. Of course, a spouse, especially a wife, may grow into the status of the partner, and men sometimes enjoy their wives' money. But even these tendencies to take advantage of the position or the wealth of the mate indicate a more personal and general aim, reaching far beyond the apparent social or economic objectives. There are men foolish enough to marry because marriage seems to them cheaper than entertaining girl friends for sexual gratification. No one can escape paying the price for what he receives; therefore, having hoped to buy more cheaply, he generally ends in feeling cheated. But the real reason why people marry, regardless of their conscious reason, is a deep desire for association, the fundamental human need to "belong," a social drive which is part of human nature.

As personality has developed in the efforts of the child to integrate himself with others, so our resulting life style attracts us to persons who fit in with our personal method of social interrelation. Sexuality and the social institution of marriage make the marital choice more intimate than any other human relationship; hence the fundamental structure of the individual personality is evinced more decisively in the choice of a mate than in any other human affiliation.

LOVE AT FIRST SIGHT

Our ability to detect, in a brief moment, the personality of another person, and to determine—although unconsciously—that he fits into our plans, is proved by the well-known phenomenon of love at first sight. Just as any homosexual knows instantly when he meets another, so we all sense immediately how far someone else corresponds to our demands.

A young woman, very attractive and intelligent, was married to a wealthy business man who was deeply devoted to her. They had a fine home and a young child whom they both worshiped. The marriage seemed to be rather successful and satisfactory. She was an active woman and he gave her full leeway. She made frequent trips all over Europe, in the company of her child. On one of these trips, she was thrown completely off balance—she never could understand how it could have hap-

87

pened. She met a man and immediately fell in love with him, so deeply that she gave up everything for him—her husband, her home, even her beloved child. To increase her perplexity, the fellow who caused all this excitement was a rather simple, dull, and by no means handsome man. He had an unstable job as a pianist in a band, and only an average education. He was incapable of any deep emotion. He was a poor choice for any girl, and no one could understand what had attracted her to him. She herself certainly could not explain it. It was just one of those mysteries of love.

After she had suffered considerably and the man had left her despite all her sacrifices, she came for psychiatric help. The analysis of her history solved the riddle. She was the only child of a wealthy father who devoted his life to her. As a child, she got whatever she wanted. So she always wanted more and got it. Her desire to excel and be worshiped was equaled only by her deep doubt of herself. She demanded continuous proof of her superiority over others. This was necessary to quiet her constant feeling of inadequacy, as she had never done any work or gained any success and recognition through contributive effort. Therefore, when her husband proposed to her, in her late teens, she accepted him as fitting perfectly into her scheme. His devotion acknowledged her superiority, his income offered her not only social status but also the gratification of her every wish.

Her efforts to test her power over him were limitless. The more she demanded, the less she gave—and he submitted. She left him alone for months, traveling throughout the world, not because of a desire for adventure—she was bored anyway—but because she could in this way test her husband's submission. But the more he gave in, the less contented she became. She began to resent her dependence on his graciousness. While she tried to dominate him, he actually grew bigger and she became insignificant. Yet she never permitted herself to become too deeply involved in other men's admiration, because her morals also served to maintain her superiority. At length she met this pianist who swept her off her feet.

Now it is not difficult to understand what attracted her. Here she found a person to whom she was really superior in every respect. She made full use of this possibility, which she recognized instinctively at their first encounter. She depended on none of *his* actions. Her superiority was based on her own contribution. Of course she could not do very much, for she was not trained. Her contributions were merely her sacrifices; her giving was giving up: child, husband, home, social life, and hundreds of conveniences. This very good-looking, wealthy woman entered the life of this nobody like a goddess. He was flattered and accepted her as a gift from heaven. But when her demands began, he flatly renounced any obligations on his side. Quarrels resulted. For a while she could keep him under thumb. But he rebelled against her tyranny and felt, quite rightly, abused. His desertion meant the final collapse of her striving for superiority. Her style of life had to be changed to bring her back into life and society.

This case demonstrates not only how much a person can realize about another in a moment's time, but also how secret tendencies lead to a particular choice. How, then, can we be sure we choose the right person? First, we must remember that love and marriage represent only one problem of life. Our attitudes toward the other sex correspond to our general approach toward life—toward any problem with which life confronts us. If we move in the right direction— in accord with the evolution and the direction of courage and social interest, in the direction of cooperation with others, of contributing and of solving our problems—then our choice will automatically be a right one. If, however, our direction is wrong, how can we expect to choose wisely? In the question of choosing a mate, our entire personal adjustment is tested.

FEELINGS ARE NO MORE THAN DEPENDABLE SERVANTS

Our feelings are always truly representative of our general line of motion. We can trust our own feelings in the sense that they will bring exactly what we expect. They may lead us into misery, but that is not their fault; they are only servants that fulfill their masters' demands. The responsible masters are our intentions and expectations, our outlook on life. Our actions—and our choice of a mate is one of them—can make us conscious of our direction. Do we love someone for his failings or for his virtues? Do we choose him because we expect protection or other material advantages, or because we understand each other? Is our love based merely on the pleasure we derive from it, or on the feeling of human closeness? Such questions may make us aware of faulty attitudes and induce us to question and change our outlook on life.

IS REASON A SOUND BASIS FOR CHOOSING?

Now there arises the question of what role reason should play in the choice of a mate. Since our feelings do not give assurance of right direction, one may be inclined to prefer reason to love as a basis for marriage. Reason cannot serve, however, unless supported by emotion. If a choice is wholesome and based on social and cooperative tendencies, the emotions will follow. Perhaps such emotion will not be so tempestuous and overwhelming as a passion that has to conquer common sense and objections and glorify an unsound choice. Feelings which comply with our reason are of a different kind; quiet affection and deep fondness seem a more reliable basis than violent fervor. But a choice not backed by any feeling can never be reasonable, because calculating schemes indicate personal rejection. The partner who is chosen only by reason, without arousing any

90

feelings, not even a strong feeling of sympathy, thereby proves himself to be unsuitable. He is chosen probably for coveted distance. Such a marriage offers plenty of distance, as it does not produce closeness, warmth, or surrender. Occasionally, however, the spiritual and emotional aloofness used as a defense mechanism by the "reasonable" partner may be abandoned in the course of marriage if a clever mate succeeds in developing confidence and courage.

This type of union was almost the rule in former times when marriage, planned by the all-important parents, was generally based on convenience. For centuries, love did not precede marriage, but developed after the wedding. In our era, one of personal independence, a person who enters marriage with an attitude of cold calculation is usually waiting for an opportunity to fall in love—with someone else. Such an "unforeseen" passion serves then very well to create and maintain an even greater marital distance, offsetting any effort from the other spouse to win more sincere cooperation.

It is impossible to say whether love or reason is a more reliable basis for a happy marriage for each without the other indicates a faulty attitude. Love in itself is definitely not trustworthy if it fails to manifest its constructive tendencies by its conformity to logic and reason; and reason becomes unreasonable if not accompanied by sincere feelings. These simple truths would be more easily recognized and the question of reason versus love would not arise so frequently if our generation were not puzzled by the present changes in our culture, especially in the relationship of the sexes. The new independence of the individual in general, and of women in particular, creates a longing for a "freedom" which actually is rather reluctance to accept obligations than real independence. The emphasis on love is less a desire to accept a person of the other sex completely than an excuse for rejecting anyone who does not arouse our love.

RUNNING AWAY FROM MARRIAGE

Without recognizing their wrong attitudes, many men and women try frantically to find a partner—and keep on trying; and so many remain lonely and companionless. They cannot, or at least they do not, love; they belong to no one, and no one belongs to them. Seldom do they recognize the actual reasons for their *success* in avoiding marriage. One girl blames her poverty, another her wealth. The poor girl bewails the fact that her lack of attractive clothing and her inability to entertain friends are responsible for her not meeting the right man; the wealthy girl complains that all men want only her money and not herself. One girl considers herself too ugly to attract any man, and another one laments her good looks as the source of her disappointments. Actually girls are sometimes refused jobs because they are too beautiful. Beautiful girls are often inclined to disregard the attention of men as an expression of personal appreciation; they feel misused, because no one is interested in their thoughts and ideas—only in their glamour.

These reasons may sound good, but not one is true. There are poor and wealthy girls happily married; ugly ones who manage to get very handsome boys, and beautiful ones who can make a success of their marriage. The fallacy is more apparent when one girl considers herself too short, and another puts the blame altogether on her height—one on her nose, the other on a slight curvature of her spine, or some other insignificant defect.

Men find equally good reasons for their inability to find mates, although, living in a man's world, they are still the choosing buyers. Consequently, they seldom put the blame on their personal shortcomings, but rather on financial or family circumstances and, most frequently, on the short-comings of the other sex. As women acquire equal status with men and imitate masculine methods, they too become critical and tend to explain their loneliness upon the lack of eligible men. In reality, they all, men and women alike, are only timid and discouraged. They fear marriage as a test which they do not expect to meet successfully. They demand security from the partner because they have none within themselves. This is the basis of their hypercritical attitude and short-lived interest. Their requirements are too great—no quality or asset can actually guarantee comfort and convenience.

LOOKING FOR PERFECTION

Their attitude is well expressed in the following episodes:

Two men met on the street. "Hello, Bob. What's the matter with you? Why do you look so down in the mouth?" Bob confessed he had just met the girl he had always been looking for: the perfect woman. He raved about her beauty, charm, intelligence, good-nature and understanding, her modesty. And she was wealthy, too. Finally the friend interrupted. "What's the matter, then?" "Nothing's wrong but my bad luck. She's looking for the perfect man!"

Do "perfect" men and women exist? A lecturer once explained that perfection cannot be found, and to demonstrate his statement, he asked his audience whether anyone had ever heard of a perfect woman. No one had. Or of a perfect man? And here

93

a small, thin voice arose. "Yes, sir, I heard of one." In a corner stood a little fellow, meek and subdued. "So you heard of a perfect man?" the speaker said. "Who was it?" And the voice came back, "My wife's first husband."

Perfection never exists in reality but only in our dreams and, if we are foolish enough to think so, in the past. But the notion of perfection is very real and has tremendous power in disparaging whatever is actually at hand.

DESIRES VERSUS REAL INTENTIONS

A very strong desire to marry does not indicate a sincere intention. It is actions that count.

A young girl had, from earliest childhood, daydreamed of her future role as a happy wife and mother. Daydreams usually indicate a situation which is considered unattainable. Confidence leads to action, not to dreams. Why did the girl distrust her matrimonial future? She was deeply discouraged by the unhappy marriage of her parents and had, since childhood, been convinced of woman's humiliating role in marriage. Her actual opinion, belying her dreams and intentions, was expressed when she warned her best friend against ever marrying. Although she thought her reasons for this advice excellent, she herself definitely intended to marry as soon as possible. Against the counsel of her friends and relatives, she became involved with a young man whom she expected to marry her.

Years passed—the young man showed less and less inclination to marry, and finally left her when she considered herself beyond marriageable age. She never really knew why, among all those who had courted her, she should have stuck to this particular man. Can it be doubted that she, who concealed a tremendous fear of marriage behind vaunted eagerness, had discovered quite early a similar deep-seated aversion to marriage in the young man? One instance finally proved her unconscious tendency to avoid marriage. She could never account for her submission to a sexual relationship with the man just before they parted. She denied any intention of attempting to hold his affection by gratifying his sexual desire. She knew the

94

affair was over. Why then did she relax her moral inhibitions just at the time when nothing could be hoped for any more? It was her "moral suicide." Now she assumed that she had forfeited her right to marry any decent and suitable man. She had established a new and lasting alibi by her "downfall." After successful therapy she changed her personal attitudes toward men and marriage and later was happily married.

OPPOSING MARRIAGE

In addition to those who profess a desire to marry without ever moving in the right direction, there are a great number who openly admit their intention to avoid marriage. Some of them make a virtue of their failure; they decry the whole institution of marriage and regard free love and promiscuity as an expression of a heroic life. Thereby, they turn cowardice into heroism. Some men denounce femininity as the cause of every evil or as something negligible or contemptible. Times when men must strive very hard to maintain their masculine superiority are characterized by a general increase of homosexual tendencies (as in ancient Greece, when growing democracy demanded feminine equality). Women who want to manifest their superiority as women are also ready for homosexual experiences, comforting each other by describing man as a brutal, insensitive, and boorish animal. Sexual perversions express a desire to avoid "normal" sexual relationships; that is, they indicate flight from the opposite sex.[4] In cases where the

[4] Perversions, especially homosexuality, are, at present, subjects of controversial scientific discussion. Some attribute them to biological abnormalities; others to a disturbance of sexual energy. Our experience with homosexual patients has proved that, although they are the most recalcitrant to therapy, their perversion is curable if we succeed in changing the patient's fundamental conception of the masculine and feminine roles. The reluctance of the patient derives from a strong feeling of justification for his

retreat is not complete, impotence and frigidity may develop. These do not hinder interest, affection, and even sexual attraction, but make complete union, at least in its physical sense, impossible.

HOW TO FIND THE RIGHT MATE

Failure to choose a mate always results in personal unhappiness, frustration, and self-isolation. Although loneliness is not limited to unmarried persons, remaining single adds disappointment and discomfort.

The puzzling question for many is how to find the right mate or how to know whether a person is a good choice. Unfortunately, there is no formula to follow. By following one's own likes and dislikes, one keeps in line with one's personality; what else can we do? We must reconcile ourselves to the fact that whatever we find is as good as we deserve. The problem is less the adequacy of the other person than one's own ability and willingness to do the best with what one is and what one has. Great is the confusion in regard to who is the right person. This confusion is augmented by literature, theatre, and movies. Poetic, religious, and romantic concepts contribute to the assumption that "marriage is made in heaven," that destiny—nothing less will suffice!—throws people together and that no force can stop it. So people wait and wait for their "destiny"—and

perverted interest. This conviction successfully conceals his elusive and retreating tendencies and helps to maintain the heroic but unfortunate role in which he takes pride. If he suffers sufficiently, then he is ready for therapy, and no biological aberrations stand in the way of recovery. As to "latent homosexuality," the phrase seems meaningless when we realize that human sexuality is fundamentally amorphous, without definite shape, and can be directed toward any gratification which the individual is willing to seek.

either do not find it or fail to recognize it. Simply because there is no one who is made to order. There is no person in the whole world just waiting as one half for the other half to complete his life. Whenever one falls in love, one thinks that this is the right one. If that were true, not so many would wake up from their dreams with headaches. The right person is a daydream, patterned by ideals, poetry, magic, and mysticism. Science is trying to prove that one choice can be better than another one.[5] The findings are less romantic than practical. Social background, educational congruity, church attendance, and common interests are no mystical preordinations. According to scientific investigations, a great many persons of the opposite sex are a good and fitting choice; and even the unfavorable choice implies only a lesser probability for marital happiness—not an impossibility. The main factor for proper choice is the willingness to choose at all—plus common sense and determination to make the best of what one gets. Those who act accordingly will always have found the right mate—the others will never be satisfied.

The less courage one has the poorer will be the choice, since then one looks more for excuses than for chances. But every choice permits some favorable chance. No person is utterly bad—as nobody is the perfect ideal. All depends upon what we see and bring out in our partner.

CORRECTING A POOR CHOICE

Can two persons living in an unhappy marriage correct the mistake of their poor choice by undoing it, or will they

[5] Ernest W. Burgess and Leonard S. Cottrell, *The Prediction of Success or Failure in Marriage.* Prentice-Hall, New York, 1939.

only commit a new blunder by breaking the human relationship which they have already established? It is easier to cut existing marital ties than to bind new and better ones. The ensuing task of choosing again will not be easier than trying to adjust oneself to the present situation. We ourselves are the source of success or failure. We cannot escape from ourselves and so cannot improve our living conditions by running away. If our relationship with the other sex is unfortunate, we must start to discover our own selves. If one freezes in a loveless marriage, he need not seek a new mate to arouse his feelings; he can try to rediscover his present mate and, with more understanding, the second choice of the same person may prove to be more fortunate. There are conditions where separation offers the only possibility of personal survival, but divorce does not always indicate incompatibility. Many marriages could be saved and many an erroneous choice transformed into the right one if people understood better how to live together.

V.

LIVING TOGETHER

THE LOGIC OF SOCIAL LIVING

To THE psychologist all marital problems present themselves in two aspects. The first is concerned with the individuals involved and their personalities, the second with the technique and methods they use in dealing with each other. It is possible to recognize the reasons for a person's actions and the nature of his difficulties by understanding his personal development, his pattern of life, his training, and the degree of his comprehension; and similarly, since all difficulties are social in character, and any difficulty in an individual's experience is, therefore, not his exclusive concern, it is necessary to recognize the human interactions and interrelationships which produce existing conditions and social atmospheres. Alfred Adler was the first to expose all individual problems and conflicts in their essentially social nature. In trying to understand the individual patients, he discovered the "logic of communal life," [1] also termed the "ironclad logic of living together," which the

[1] Alfred Adler, *Understanding Human Nature*. Greenberg Publishers, New York, 1927.

99

neurotic patient disregards and offends. He formulated certain laws which must be observed in group living, wherever people wish to get along with each other. Definite rules of cooperation are essential for the preservation of every harmonious human relationship. All failures in life, all unhappiness and disappointment can be traced back to disregard and violation of the necessary rules of cooperation.

What does cooperation mean? Is it, as many seem to think, a moral obligation of our fellow-man toward ourselves? We easily realize its absence in others, and we recognize then its importance. But it is difficult to perceive deficiency of cooperation in ourselves. Although we have definite ideas of what cooperation means, we apply them only in limited degree to ourselves.

THE SCIENCE OF COOPERATION

Cooperation as a subject for research seems to imply the consideration of values which appertain less to science than to religion and ethics. It is easy for the physical sciences to ignore values. Psychology, however, cannot do this, for its very subject is the person who evaluates. It must deliberately attempt to make bias a subject of research, and even accept its presence in the research procedure and find some means of overcoming its undesirable effects. Psychology as a science must remain free from subjectivity as far as is humanly possible; it must refrain from personal evaluation —but it must analyze it.

We can avoid irrelevant and undesirable evaluation when we define cooperation without reference to morals and ethics, by not seeking to determine whether a particular act is "good" or "bad." In pointing out the results to which a specific act will lead, however, we remain objective and can achieve a good description of cooperation.

Those acts which disturb human relationship we may regard as contradictory to the rules of cooperation. All those acts which tend to remove friction and antagonism from human relationships seem to be in accord with the rules of cooperation. Cooperation is orderly interaction, harmonious working together toward a common objective, agreement and mutual assistance. All those acts which stimulate or increase these conditions can be considered as conforming with the rules of cooperation, and whatever creates disagreement, friction, and opposition, as violating them. A clear knowledge of these rules can help considerably to improve vital cooperation and to avoid disastrous mistakes. Investigation of all factors involved is not yet concluded. We can hope to obtain a clearer picture through the integrated research of psychology, social science, and probably anthropology. Already, however, we know some of the fundamentals upon which cooperation is based. For marital happiness especially, observance of the rules of cooperation is imperative, since marriage is the closest kind of living together—the most intimate association between two human beings.

Human nature is essentially social, and human qualities result from social intercourse. Human beings isolated for a period of years—a shipwrecked sailor, for example—lose all typical human qualities. Responsiveness to interhuman contact, however, is based on an innate social feeling. This, the result of several hundred thousand years of community living, is inherited as a potentiality and must be developed

101

anew in each child to the high degree necessary for the intricate social order of our present culture. The ability to cooperate is based primarily on the amount of social feeling which a person has developed during childhood and after.

Social feeling means social interest; it is the expression of a sense of belonging together. Lack of sufficient social feeling limits cooperation; fellow men too easily appear to be sinister antagonists against whom defense is imperative. The resulting feeling of hostility prevents cooperation just as social feeling establishes it.

The feeling of belonging presupposes confidence in others, who are recognized and accepted as fellow creatures, and confidence in oneself as a source of strength which enables us to face any eventuality. Fear is the chief obstacle to cooperation. Human beings develop social feelings and act cooperatively as long as fear does not frustrate their natural inclinations. The desire to cooperate is curbed only by a feeling of inferiority which produces a compulsion toward self-defense. Very frequently the defensive attitude is assumed unnecessarily in the face of an imaginary danger, usually when one senses a threat to personal prestige. Everyone prefers to cooperate and suffers if he cannot.

Since fear is the chief obstacle to cooperation, how can we avoid it? Apparently the establishment of a feeling of security is one means. But security in itself does not exist. Death, sickness, and disaster threaten constantly—and always will. We cannot establish security because we cannot perfectly control these threats. We can, however, cultivate confidence in ourselves and our neighbors. We can cultivate whatever gives us acceptance in their eyes and find acceptable whatever we can in the qualities they present. Only self-confidence can help us face eventualities beyond our control. Self-confidence evinced under stress is courage. Courage and self-confidence constitute the only possible basis for a feeling of security, founded on the realization that whatever may arise, one will be able to take it and to make the best of it.

THE FUNDAMENTAL ATTITUDES TOWARD OR AGAINST COOPERATION

Thus we see two opposing groups of qualities, or attitudes:

Social feeling	Hostility
Confidence in others	Distrust and suspicion
Self-confidence	Inferiority feelings
Courage	Fear

Social feeling means confidence in others, which is impossible without confidence in oneself, expressed in courage. These four qualities are the fundamental source of cooperative action, whereas their antagonists are the general causes for non-cooperation. From these fundamental attitudes, certain behavior patterns result, which we superficially designate as character traits. Hatred, envy, jealousy, preemptoriness, conceit, and deprecativeness are defense mechanisms employed by an individual to fortify his unwillingness to participate in his social group. Leniency, good-heartedness, generosity, and tolerance, on the other hand, express cooperative tendencies.

Two misconceptions result from a wrong idea of human cooperation. One is the belief that resentment can lead to improvement or that it is even a prerequisite for actions directed toward improvement. People unaware of the psychological structure of resentment—its origin, its consequences—are liable to overlook the fact that resentment means a hostile emotion directed *against* something unpleasant. But do we need hostile emotions to remedy disagreeable situations and conditions? Most people are inclined to believe so. How wrong they are! Constructive changes do not require hostility. On the contrary, hostile actions generally disturb more than they improve, because they result in more friction and disagreement. We do not develop hostile feelings for the sake of improvement. Hostility appears only when we lose confidence in our success. As long as one believes that he can accomplish a change, he will not resent the original predicament; but as soon as doubt arises in the final solution, resentment begins. Although a wife may dislike her husband's habits, as long as there is any hope that he may change she will not feel resentful. Her resentment expresses her growing discouragement. As resentment is based on fear and lack of confidence, it prevents a satisfactory solution. Actual improvement cannot be accomplished without acceptance. This term again requires clarification.

Acceptance is not identical with agreement. If we accepted only when we fully approved, there would remain very little for us to accept. No person has only qualities which we like, but does that mean that we cannot accept anyone? Acceptance includes more than concord. It is the expression of a positive attitude toward something or someone, regardless of existing shortcomings and deficiencies. Our ability to influence requires a friendly and understanding attitude. Only then are we able to influence people toward improved cooperation; only then can we develop constructive plans to overcome obstacles. The husband will gladly adjust himself to his wife's desires if he feels fully accepted by her, but he may drive in the opposite direction if he senses her resentment and rejection.

The second misconception about the principles of co-operation lies in the general belief that when interests clash, nothing can be done except to fight or yield. Yet, in either case cooperation will be destroyed and nothing will be won. Yielding means submission, humiliation, and ultimately rebellion and opposition. Fighting and warfare generally end in suppression. Here, too, hatred appears in the vanquished, and fearful insecurity in the victor. There are situations which seem to necessitate fighting. But such situations are already the consequence of previous hostilities. Fighting itself never ends hostilities. It only concludes certain phases of the warfare for limited periods of time. Even if it brings victory momentarily, by fighting back we only prepare for the next outburst of more or less open hostilities, unless we are capable of establishing a new relationship of equality and mutual confidence.

As this is true of the relationship between nations and groups, so is it between parents and children, husbands and wives. Few of our contemporaries are prepared to meet divergent interests in a cooperative spirit. Their lack of social feeling, courage, and confidence is responsible for their fallacious conviction that a solution can be found by fighting or yielding. A proper attitude is necessary to settle controversies without violation of the dignity and self-respect of the persons involved. Although human beings have lived together for very long, we are still illiterates in the art of living together. Democracy, appearing on the horizon of human society five or six thousand years ago, is still an ideal which has to be realized. Psychology and psychiatry can promote democratic relationships by analyzing and correcting individuals and their interrelationships.

RELATIONSHIPS ARE BASED ON INTERACTIONS

Whatever happens between two human beings is the expression of a certain equilibrium established soon after they first meet, and subject only to periodic changes. These changes rarely alter the structure of the relationship; they are mainly modifications or shifting of methods. No incident affecting the relationship, however disturbing or pleasant, can be attributed to one side alone. Both parties continuously play into each other's hands, regardless how active the one and how passive the other may seem. The tormentor is not more guilty than the martyr who permits the cruelty to continue, the torment to recur. Tyranny in marriage cannot be maintained without indulgent submission; courage and self-respect always stop it.

Unfortunately, since no one knows himself, the parties involved rarely recognize their own contribution and their provocative influence on each other. This interrelationship and mutual goading result in a more complicated picture when the family circle includes more persons—children or relatives. A definite equilibrium exists all the time, maintained by a secret and unconscious agreement between all members. If one person in the group fundamentally changes his position, his habits, his attitudes, or character, the

106

change has far-reaching effects on each member of the family, strongest upon those with whom he was locked in some kind of competition, which is an equilibrium held in suspension. Allies as a rule have a firmer platform upon which they can stand together. The equilibrium between competitors and antagonists is a more delicate one, continuously challenged and restored, but continuously maintained. This is the type of equilibrium which leads to a constant change of methods and emotions, as each party responds vigorously to the slightest turn of the other. Moods of amiability and anger may alternately reach such extremes as overt acceptance or rejection.

Unfortunately, this chaotic intercourse is a prominent characteristic of our present-day family life, where mutual competition is a standard relationship between man and wife, parents and children, older and younger siblings. Consequently, each problem or conflict disturbing the peace of the family cannot be understood "logically" from the point of view of who is right and who is wrong. We must realize the psychological meaning of the problem in regard to the persons who create it. It makes no difference whether the conflicts are minor and trivial or decisive and disastrous; we must distinguish between the logical content and the psychological meaning. And the solution must be concerned as much with the general rules of human conduct as with the psychological structures of the principals.

LOGICAL MERIT VERSUS PSYCHOLOGICAL SIGNIFICANCE

Here is a simple example of an incident which might occur in any family:

The husband comes home from work, fatigued, after some unpleasant experience at his office. The wife has been home all day, looking forward to the evening, planning to go with him to visit some friends. He refuses. He is too tired. She retorts, "Yes, I know. You are always too tired when I want to go out. This time I insist that you come with me." And the quarrel is on its way. She will cry or sulk, and he may give in at the end, dress up, and go out with her. But that is no solution, whether they go out or stay home. If he submits, he feels victimized and, angry as he is, can scarcely enjoy the party. If, on the other hand, he fights persistently, they probably argue all evening, and perhaps spend a sleepless night, awakening in the morning, ready for the next fight.

All the elements of a typical conflict can be recognized in this little incident. Cooperation is definitely disturbed, but it would be incorrect to blame either husband or wife and their conflicting interests. If husband and wife were on good terms, the feeling would not arise in each of them that the other has no understanding and shows no consideration. Logically, both are justified in their demands. But it makes no difference who is right or wrong. If they were friendly with each other, they could easily find an agreement according to the importance of each one's desire. If the visit is an exceptional occasion, the husband can overcome his tiredness and perhaps even enjoy the distraction. And if his exhaustion and discouragement are considerable, the devoted wife might prefer to comfort him rather than to visit with casual friends. If the importance of the visit and the exhaustion of the husband are both extraordinary, it might be difficult to decide, but a decision which leads to a quarrel won't lessen the pressure. Each one's willingness to see the other's point of view is more

108

likely to lead to an agreement than each one's defense of his own.

The psychological meaning of the problem may, however, lie deeper—in the husband's general reluctance for social contact, and in the wife's inability to make her life enjoyable and worthwhile during the day. Or it may be that she is of a demanding type, not satisfied that the husband provides the money and support, but desirous of his full attention and time when he is not engaged in spending them for his wife's sustenance. The incident described is then merely an occasion for the deeper resentment to flare up.

Whenever any conflict arises, the first decision which both parties make—definitely, although unconsciously—is whether to use these incidents as an occasion to fight, for hurting and being hurt, or whether to try sincerely to solve the problem. If the tendency is to quarrel, there can be no solution before one of them checks this inclination. Here we meet one of the most important obstacles to married happiness: the general belief that something can be gained by fighting. So both blame and scold and get excited—and prepare the field for the next fight. They are less interested in finding a solution than in being "right."

Winning or losing this one fight will not help. What would help is social feeling—the feeling of belonging together—which makes every conflict a common problem, not a question of what he wants or she wants. Social feeling creates a "we" of which he and she are each only one part. Conflicting interests become opportunities for asserting unity through mutual effort, establishing conditions which both can enjoy together—in this case, either in staying at home or in going out. Confidence in each other stimulates mutual trust and willingness to assist each other. If he puts his interest in her hands, she is more likely to consider his desires rather than her own. This is especially true for children who voluntarily change stony stubbornness into willing consideration if they are asked what should be done. Adults are not much different.

VETO STRONGER THAN DEMAND

Many people believe force helps. If they cannot force the issue physically, as too often they do with their children, they do it morally or mentally. Here we must recognize the aggressive character of force as contrasted with the nonviolent passive resistance. Active forcing always means violating respect for someone else. Resistance, on the other hand, is seldom an imposition; it merely preserves respect for oneself. The old Romans expressed a fine understanding for rules of cooperation when they demanded that their two Consuls could only act when both agreed. The veto of one was always stronger than the demand of the other. What one wanted did not count when the other disliked it. That should be a rule for family life as well. In our case, it is the wife who wants to go out, while the husband prefers to stay home; it is she who wants to *do* something and he doesn't like it. His veto should be stronger than her demand. It means more hardship for him to do what he does not like than for her to refrain from what she likes very much, unless, of course, she is able to win him over.

Unfortunately, the ancient rule of the veto is rarely applied, as most people find it difficult to distinguish between imposing upon and merely not yielding. If they do

110

not get what *they want,* they feel abused and coerced. (This attitude is typical of pampered children; its prevalence among adults is an indication of how few are actually grown up.) In the event of conflicting interests it seems advisable to let everyone do what he likes: not to impose, but not to permit imposition either. Only too often do we fail to recognize the distinction between the two and the practical applications of this principle. Behind this difficulty lies the lack of respect so often found between the closest relatives. They just do not respect each other, despite all their unquestionable love and devotion.

SOURCES OF MUTUAL DISRESPECT

There are many reasons why people so often find it difficult to treat other members of the family with proper respect. Whatever the reason is, it can be traced to personal fears and inferiority feelings. We all are inclined to be more critical of the shortcomings of relatives because we identify ourselves with them. Their shortcomings reflect on our own value and status. We feel ashamed of their faults, as if they were our own. If we were more sure of ourselves, of our own value and position, we could accept our own shortcomings and those of our close associates more readily, because we would not consider them as expressions of our value and significance. A self-confident person is able to regard faults, limitations, and shortcomings in their proper perspective, without unduly making them tests of social value. Respect for members of one's family is, therefore, closely linked with self-respect. He who fears disgrace and humiliation in the world at large becomes over-sensitive of his relatives' imperfections. Moreover, if one feels helpless

111

in regard to such shortcomings, one resents them and expresses resentment, either passively and sullenly or in an openly violent and aggressive way. Both lead to disrespect of the dignity and worth of the others.

Another reason for the lack of respect within many families is the existing state of competition in which we live, in the outside world as well as within our intimate family circle. We have already described why husbands and wives of today generally regard each other as competitors. Children, too, are definitely in competition with each other. They fight for their parents' love and attention. Each regards the other as a threat to his own position, developing a deep sense of competitive strife, and overcoming each other in turn—often, by this means, introducing an element of unrest and friction in family life. The same competition exists between parents and children. The two generations carry on a family fight, too, for prestige. In a world which grants so little security and certainty of personal appreciation, parents naturally try to impress with their own superiority those who seem to offer the least resistance. Many parents do not recognize the acts of hostility and combat which are so often disguised as exuberant love and overwhelming affection. Humiliation and worship color the relationships of parents and children more frequently than do respect and human dignity. It would be worthwhile to treat our relatives and children—and parents—as we would treat casual acquaintances whom we meet socially. We are all rather well trained to meet antagonistic interests in society, politely and with due respect for each other. Couldn't we use this technique and knowledge also in our own family?

INTIMACY CAN HAMPER FRIENDLINESS

Family ties alone do not guarantee friendly relationship. Wooing and charming are no less necessary after the wedding than before, notwithstanding the mistaken adage regarding the futility of chasing a streetcar after one has caught it. On the contrary, close association demands more consideration and understanding for the preservation of friendship and affection. It is much easier to get along with people whom we see rarely. Distance facilitates harmony. It is necessary in marriage to accept and like each other, even unwashed and unkempt. But why must we take more pains to appeal to perfect strangers or casual friends than to those for whom we care the most? Parents make the same mistake when they expect their children's love merely because they have begotten them. The devotion and respect of children must also continuously be won anew. A friendly atmosphere within the family is evident in many ways. The tone of voice in which father, mother, and children address each other reveals whether friendliness and respect reign, or friction and humiliation and force. We should sharpen our ears to realize these subtle signs of disturbed cooperation. Unfortunately, we cannot hear ourselves as we sound to others. A discovery which would enable us to do so would certainly merit the Nobel Peace Prize.

INTIMIDATION INSTEAD OF FIRMNESS

Kindness, however, does not exclude firmness. On the contrary, one can be kind only if one is sure of oneself, sure of the impression one makes, and sure of the final success. To be firm requires the same self-confidence. Firmness does not imply imposition. The less firm and sure we are, the more we tend to intimidate and impose. This mutual intimidation is only too often found in family life. Of course, we do not inject fear deliberately, but we ourselves are certainly afraid. Like two men unexpectedly meeting at midnight on a dark street, each afraid that the other wants to rob him, neither suspecting that the other one, too, is shivering in fear, many a husband and wife live in fear, the fear of being neglected, of not being appreciated, of being dominated or abused, frustrated or humiliated. They will admit their fears confidentially to a third person, but it is difficult to convince either that the other is afraid, too. None recognizes the fears of his opponent, especially in regard to relative superiority; we are all inclined to suspect others of being, or at least attempting to be, superior to us. Of course, the methods and weapons of warfare are clearly recognized as such only if used by our opponent; we consider ourselves harmless and full of good intentions, denying others any reason for self-defense with regard to us.

LOGIC USED AS A WEAPON

All marital quarrels show fundamentally the same structure. Listening to husband and wife, one feels sure that the one who talked last is right. And they are both right—or at least they believe they are. Otherwise, they would act differently. Logic becomes only a weapon which can be used, and is used, by everyone who fights. But fundamentally, the quarrel is never a question of right or wrong— only of pleasing or antagonizing, of agreeing or opposing. The bone of contention plays, generally, a secondary and accidental role. The issue of right or wrong arises only

114

THE CHALLENGE OF MARRIAGE

when cooperation is disturbed and each wants to shift the blame for the discord. Human beings are remarkably clever and astonishingly adept at finding reasons to justify their actions. Their scheming minds invent slight provocations to incite the other to more drastic actions which then are justifiable causes for open hostility.

DEMANDING INSTEAD OF WINNING

Methods of pleasing are easily available, but are far less frequently utilized. When we want to please we are all able to do so, although some are so discouraged that they have stopped trying, desperate of ever being liked. We all have hundreds of little ways to show affection and to attract it. Yet in family life we insist on legal rights first and try to get before we are willing to give. Otherwise we feel abused. If we do not get what we want, or what we believe we deserve, we punish, although in that way we diminish the readiness of the other one to do his share.

SHIFTING THE BLAME

Since we do not know ourselves, or admit our real intentions, or hear the way we sound, or realize when we provoke, how can we be sure whether we violate the fundamental rules of cooperation or observe them? We are able to evaluate ourselves properly only if we look at the consequences of our actions. Then we may determine whether we are provoking more friction and tension or promoting a better understanding. This procedure, however, demands that we abandon all hope of putting the blame for any family discord on factors outside ourselves. Nor will blaming ourselves help. Blame, excuses, complaints—all indicate discouragement and resentment. Whenever we detect in ourselves any sign of such inclinations, we can be sure that we are going to violate rules of cooperation. Our own emotions are good guides, if we regard them as indications of our own intentions, and not, as many foolishly do, as a natural "reaction" to stimulation from the outside. Taking full responsibility for our emotions deprives us of easy excuses, but it enables us to gain mastery of the situation. When we recognize hostile emotions as deliberate weapons of warfare, they may stimulate a reorientation, a new evaluation of living conditions and family members, so that new emotions, more benevolent and more courageous, may develop. Properly understood, the alleged lack of affection will no longer be an excuse for neglected human duties but a challenge to develop a new social interest.

Innumerable reasons are given for falling out of love. One woman complained that she could no longer love and accept her husband, for the reason that he had absolutely no faults. "You can't imagine how terrible it is to live with a man who is perfect. I really can't stand it any longer. If he did something wrong only once! If he would be angry with me! But no, whatever I do is all right. Whatever I don't do is all right, too. He never loses his temper. Can you live with an angel?" Unbelievable as it may sound, one hears such a complaint not infrequently. It only shows that if someone wants to find a reason for opposing, he always can. A lack of fault serves the purpose as well as too many.

The question arises, then, of whether personal faults are the actual causes of marital friction. Is it true that we reject someone because of his faults? I do not think so. As long as we accept and love someone, his faults do not matter; when we refuse to accept him, his faults simply supply us with a good reason for our hostility. We discover faults which we readily overlooked before when they fitted into our plans. Then why do we reject each other, causing endless pain to ourselves as well as to others? It is always the question of our own importance which interferes with our happiness and our cooperation. As long as we feel recognized, appreciated, worshiped—and pampered—everything is all right. But as soon as we feel inferior and unequal, our closest friend becomes our enemy.

This feeling of inferiority generally has no actual basis, yet compensations, namely, a state of superiority, may be sought in various ways. The position of a victimized martyr may seem to any observer a state of definite inferiority and humiliation, but the person who evokes this position for himself finds in it an opportunity for moral superiority. Suffering physical and mental torture may even enhance the spiritual "victory," and martyr and torturer can get along happily on the basis of their distribution of power. One enjoys his physical dominance, and the other one his righteousness. But the martyr may immediately rebel and reject his mate should he ever attempt to be virtuous and considerate, for considerateness would spell defeat and disrupt the equilibrium. This situation is, of course, extreme, but we must keep in mind that mutual acceptance means agreement about the equilibrium which permits each party to compensate in his way for his feeling of inadequacy. Friction is never caused solely by external disturbances. Economic or social pressure or misfortune can normally bring husband and wife closer together. If the equilibrium between the couple is shaken by these hard-

117

ships, then friction results. Most frequently these adversities are not the cause of marital disturbances—they are merely a test of the ability to cooperate. They bring hidden conflicts and resentment into the open which indicate that the feeling of belonging is inadequate in both parties, and that they are unwilling to stick together through hardship. They look only for an occasion each to blame the other for the reverses.

WE DECIDE OUR RESPONSES

It is only human to become critical of others when we suffer from our own shortcomings. Then we become interested in the faults of others. Ordinarily our natural social interest enables us to see and enjoy the good qualities in our fellow men. Everyone has virtues, just as everyone has faults. Whether we emphasize his faults or his virtues indicates our attitude toward a person. That is true for human beings as for life in general; both are so rich and colorful that we can single out whatever we want—the good or the bad. It is not a question of whether disturbing or pleasing experiences are more frequent; the advantages and disadvantages we find in life and in persons reflect only our own attitudes.

How much it is up to ourselves whether we resent or accept is demonstrated by the following case:

A patient lived in a very peculiar marriage. He had had no sex relations with his wife for many years, although both were rather young. She did not excite his fancy, he said, and he disliked her physically. He made no secret of having mistresses and bragged about their gifts and other signs of enchantment. How did this equilibrium develop? He had grown up in competition with an older sister, trying from childhood on to demonstrate

118

his "masculine superiority." Unfortunately, his desire to feel that he was a strong man was never satisfied. The dominant father he tried to imitate gave him too powerful evidence of his own inadequacy. Consequently, he developed a peculiar system of tyrannizing and charming others to give in to his whims, avoiding very carefully any situation where his dreaded inferiority might become apparent. He married rather young, when he found a girl deeply devoted to him and willing to live and die for him. She was a wonderful housekeeper, and provided for him a comfortable "temple" where he was enthroned as a god.

After a few years, however, he became apprehensive and rebelled. As high priestess of the sanctuary, she exerted certain pressure on him—for his comfort and benefit, to be sure, but creating in him a sense of being pushed. Her concern for his welfare repelled him. Her moral superiority threatened him and increased his fear of being dominated. Abruptly he decided to leave her. She became hysterical and literally fell on her knees, embracing his legs, and implored him to keep her as a slave. He could do whatever he wanted, as long as she could stay with him and serve him. His feeling of superiority was saved—and he stayed. To test his power, he ignored her domestic efforts by entering the house with dirty shoes and by similar offenses. It broke her heart, but she suffered in silence. He went out with other women, not without telling her of his experiences and successes. She was hungry for his love and affection so he denied her both.

During therapy he understood his mistaken conception of superiority and the fallacy of his effort to avoid any pressure from the outside world, expressed in various nervous symptoms which had induced him to seek medical attention. One day he came in and reported, obviously amazed, an unexpected sexual relationship with his wife the night before. He did not understand himself. For many years he had considered her distasteful and sexually repulsive. How could he suddenly feel sexually attracted? Had she changed? Certainly not. It was he who had changed, not alone in his attitude toward her, but toward life in general, so that he looked at her differently and became willing to commit himself again, no longer afraid of losing status.

119

From this moment on, normal relations continued. He gave up his girl friends whose admiration—and even gifts—he no longer needed as proof of his masculine superiority.

MARRIAGE IS NO HEAVEN

It is difficult for two people to be friends day and night, to agree, and to cooperate in all turns life may take. In view of the complex and almost unsolvable problems he faces, nobody can feel thoroughly adequate. Many carry the hostility and apprehension from the external world back into the home and return to the world unrested, with increased tension. The disappointment is the greater the more one expects to find a haven in marriage. It is a grave mistake to look upon marriage as a solution. It is a *task*. People, especially women, discouraged in life, hope to find security in marriage, only to experience frightful disillusionment. In former times, marriage was a solution for a woman's problems. Without a husband, women did not count—and nothing mattered once she was married. Today it is different. Advising a discouraged girl to get married is harmful. Whoever feels inadequate in regard to work and social obligations faces failure in the even more exacting cooperation demanded from the close human relationship in marriage. Not that people should be discouraged from marrying. They cannot run away from sex and love without becoming more deeply disappointed. The point is that whatever one does in anxiety and cowardice, one has to pay for. Whether one tries to escape from marriage or to escape into marriage, the curse of cowardice follows him. Courage and social feeling, if not previously developed, must be deliberately fostered, in order to prepare for marrying or to make the best of an already contracted marriage.

120

THE SPIRIT COUNTS

It seems futile to give specific recommendations for a happy life. Many books advise what to do and what not to do. The pity is that the suggestions, regardless of how good they are, generally do not help. A courageous person with sufficient social interest does not need advice, and a fearful, hostile person will fail to heed even the best advice. There-fore, we have stressed in this chapter fundamental attitudes more than specific techniques. No technique alone can preserve marital happiness—no rule in handling economic, social, or sexual problems can prevent failure. The spirit counts, and not the technique. The willingness to cooperate can overcome every obstacle, and without this fundamental willingness, minor obstacles can become overwhelming. Whatever intensifies, between husband and wife, the feel-ing of belonging strengthens their resistance to perils threatening from within or without. Any outlook on life based on faith and confidence—religious or secular—in-creases aptitude and competence for harmonious coopera-tion and generates an atmosphere of genuine kindness and tolerance. The problems overtly blamed for the disruption of marital happiness provide only test situations through which erroneous attitudes can be brought to light.

VI.

THE fact that jealousy is very closely related to the popular conception of the role of sex indicates that the whole subject needs clarification. The meaning and implication given to fidelity and possession often disturbs the human fellowship of husband and wife and brings to a head the personal problems threatening understanding and harmony. Not only does jealousy express the competition between man and woman, man and man, and woman and woman; it intensifies the competition. Because investigation of this subject offers so many opportunities to explore the bases of many conflicts in marriage, as well as the differences between their logical and psychological content, it is profitable to use this topic as the beginning of an analysis of concrete problems.

IS JEALOUSY A SIGN OF LOVE?

It is a general belief that jealousy and love belong inseparably together, so that love without jealousy seems impossible. Jealousy is frequently regarded as a true measure of the degree and depth of love, and many realize that they

122

are in love only when they become jealous. For them, the overwhelming power of love is never more impressively revealed than by the poignant wretchedness of jealousy. They do not stop to realize how much fury, hostility, and antagonism they thus require in order to discover love. Although hardly anyone escapes the painful experience of jealousy, hardly anyone understands its true meaning and essential structure. We lose our common sense while we are in the grip of jealousy, and even after we have regained our clear and collected judgment we fail to understand its nature.

The nature of antagonistic emotions generally prohibits a conscious admission of their underlying tendencies, as these tendencies are irreconcilable with our desire to maintain a respectable opinion of ourselves. Thus we excuse one of the most vicious intentions—namely, to hurt someone we love—by referring to the most widely accepted values in life: love, devotion, chastity, and trustworthiness. The jealous person expresses his concern with these ethical and moral aspects while he neglects the most elementary rules of decency.

Let us see clearly: We can be jealous without being in love. That is true not only for the relationship between friends, between members of the family, and between two persons whose relationships are not sexually tinged; men and women slightly interested erotically in each other can become jealous without any sign of deeper devotion. A girl attracting the attention of many suitors may become distinctly jealous if one of them is in danger of being lured by the charm of another girl. On the other hand, infidelity in itself does not necessarily produce jealousy in the loving cuckold. Many a man loves his wife for her success with other men, which evokes pleasant stimulations. The psychological background of jealousy is more complicated and not at all related directly to the problem of faithfulness.

THE PROBLEM OF FIDELITY

Fidelity is one of the major problems in marriage. Although accepted as an absolute and unequivocal value and prerequisite, its realization is today more questionable and confused than ever before. At times, actual physical possession of a woman was possible—by force of a strict law (harems), or by ruthlessness (slavery). Even then the rather slight possibility of infidelity did not prevent violent jealousy. Today, possession of another person either physically or mentally is entirely impossible. There is no security whatsoever about the faithfulness of the partner. The question is even advanced whether human beings are capable of fidelity. Doubt arises especially about the monogamous nature of males. Scientists refer to the biological difference which permits a man to beget innumerable children almost consecutively, while physiological conditions limit a woman to one a year, or perhaps two—unless she is exceptional and produces quintuplets. Making a psychological distinction between men and women on the ground of difference in physiological mechanisms is always dubious procedure—generally used to justify masculine privileges.

The undeniable biological differences have small bearing on habits and customs. The biological ability of a man to have fifty children at one time means practically nothing; when he can suppress his forty-nine desires for other women, he can as well control the one remaining philandering desire to which he wants to be entitled. Feminists who would attempt to postulate the right of women to sexual licentiousness could equally well point out that one woman is capable physiologically of more sexual gratifications than any one man can provide. We must remember that conditions of human life are not governed by natural forces, like biological and physiological drives or impulses, but by social conventions. Monogamy, therefore, has nothing to do with the intrinsic structure of human nature. Man can live monogamously or polygamously—and women are a part of mankind. The development of monogamy can be explained by the establishment of civilization, with segregated families. During the evolution of mankind, the idea of the "individual" distinguishable as such from the mass, the clan, or the sib, developed. Human progress means establishment and extension of individual conceptions and drives. Monogamy resulted as the strongest union of two individuals. Christianity, historically the first concept of fundamental human equality, stipulated, in the strongest possible way, monogamy as the ideal relationship between men and women, at a time when social conditions, especially the love concept of the antique society, gave man polygamous rights as the prerogative of his supremacy.

This ideal of everlasting unbreakable devotion and loyalty has been maintained and intensified throughout the last centuries, although we are still far from achievement. Not only do social conditions and morals point toward monogamy; a deep psychological desire for complete and lasting union elevates monogamy to a dream of mankind. For psychological reasons, too, monogamy in its true sense still is more of a dream than a reality, although it is legally demanded and supervised.

CAUSES OF UNFAITHFULNESS

The problem of fidelity is confused by the uncertainty about the nature of faithfulness. From a materialistic point of view, faithfulness refers to physical chastity—an attitude necessitating very intricate and peculiar distinctions if the Christian ideal of monogamy is to be preserved under present conditions. It remains controversial where adultery starts. Some are inclined to regard a warm handshake or a deep look into each other's eyes as trespassing the limits of decent behavior. Others have no objection to a kiss or even a passionate embrace. If we include dreams and thoughts as criteria, certainly few of our ideals could be maintained. Christianity itself found a means of uniting the spiritual desire for chastity with the psychological inability of man to accomplish it. The distinction between the willingness of spirit and the weakness of flesh is only the expression of the conflict within ourselves. But does this mean that we must overpower our human nature to be faithful? Some think so. They believe in the irreconcilable antagonism between the sexual drive toward unrestricted gratification and the social obligation of chastity. In reality, the longing for sexual variety is, as we have demonstrated, as closely connected with the social aspirations as is the devotion to one person. The hostility, fear, and opposition which prevent complete devotion and surrender and create this desire for variety do not stem from sexual urges, but hostility and antagonism can utilize sexual capacities in the pursuit of anti-social tendencies. The "weak flesh" is an expression of

126

the restricted social feeling of mankind in a world which, even now, still makes it difficult for human beings to achieve close human cooperation, courage, and a sense of belonging. Psychological factors which endanger human relationships stand in the way of unconditional cooperation and unreserved mutual acceptance. They make true monogamy today rather an exception and hamper exclusive and permanent sexual and personal interest.

Our susceptibility to temptation grows out of disappointment, quarrels, and antagonism, so often occurring in marriage. The longing for variety arises not incidentally but always in direct connection with some marital conflict. Polygamous tendencies arise when a person is discouraged in his love, when he wants to withdraw, to punish, or to exhibit privileges and the rights of his sex. No individual who finds full satisfaction in his marriage looks elsewhere. But since our capacity for love is restricted by general discouragement and distress, almost everyone at some periods of life has felt the longing for variety. Especially when we grow older the desire to prove our ability to conquer and win often leads to yearning for other experience. The legal expression of this yearning is divorce, which gives opportunity for various sexual experiences without openly violating the principle of monogamy.

IS "FRIENDSHIP" BETWEEN MEN AND WOMEN POSSIBLE?

At this point a discussion of platonic friendship seems indicated. The frequency with which this question is raised indicates a general skepticism. Of course, there are some natural obstacles to such friendship. If a man and a woman

are devoted to each other, if they have many common interests, if they feel close and friendly, sex naturally in-
trudes. When this happens, we speak no longer of friendship but of love.

It is rather strange to differentiate between love and
friendship, as if they were contradictory, and as if sincere
love did not include friendship as well. However, in speaking of friendship between the sexes we mean a "platonic"
relationship, without obvious sexual attraction. One school
of thought, Freud's psychoanalysis, maintains that any kind
of sympathy and devoted personal interest, even between
two persons of the same sex, is based on a so-called latent
sexual desire. The validity of this theory is very much challenged. It certainly leaves no room for human friendship as
such. It does not explain the obvious difference between a
merely human and a sexually tinctured relationship.

The question, how far a close personal relationship
devoid of sexual interest on either side is possible between
a man and a woman, can only be answered when we recognize that we ourselves are the masters of our emotions and
can create or suppress any of them according to our inclinations. We actually can establish any kind of relationship with a person of the same or of the opposite sex. We
can either develop sexual reactions or suppress them. A
mere friendship between a man and woman can develop,
for instance, when both are in love with someone else. This
seems to be the most favorable condition for retaining a
"platonic" friendship, although any friendship between
persons of opposite sexes can be maintained without the
interference of sexual desires, if and when both are deter-

mined not to regard the other as a possible object for erotic gratification.

This fact, however, will not prevent a jealous husband or wife from resenting a true friendship between his mate and another person of the other sex. The reference to possible infidelity is only a convenient excuse, as jealousy is not restricted to the sexual sphere; jealousy can as well be aroused by members of the family, by any other outside interest of the mate, even by his work. Therefore, one-sided friendships need not disrupt or endanger marital harmony. Husbands and wives can retain their friendships as long as they trust one another, provided neither wants to possess the other completely.

THE ANSWER TO PHILANDERING

How to cultivate fidelity presents one of the most difficult problems for marital living together. Unfortunately, we are uncertain not only of our partners, but of ourselves. So long as both partners have the confidence to face problems together and squarely, no problem actually will disturb the marital relationship. No matter how difficult a problem may be—and the problem of infidelity certainly is not an easy one—it should and can be solved jointly, provided both have faith, courage, and the desire for a solution. The greater the problem which people manage to solve together, the closer grows their relationship, because in their troubles they need and may find each other. After the danger is over, a sense of gratefulness for the mutual help and under-standing deepens the all-important feeling of belonging.

Many regard jealousy as an adequate response to phi-landering tendencies in the mate. They feel there is no alternative, save to close their eyes deliberately and maintain an imperturbable ignorance that might prove to be more comfortable, but does not solve the problem. They forget that jealousy does not ever solve any problem either. Instead of bringing back the straying mate, it only increases the distance and endangers the unity. Suspicion and fear which lead inevitably to open hostility merely aggravate the problem which first tempted the mate to look outside the marriage for erotic adventures.

Shall we then ignore the danger of losing our mate? Or permit him to be unfaithful? No one could recommend that. But actually neither danger is avoided by jealousy. We can easily recognize the foolishness of a woman who is constantly afraid that her healthy husband may die someday, and envisions in every slight ailment potential complications. It seems obvious that her fear expresses other perturbations than actual concern with a possible and far-distant loss. The same is true of jealousy. The fear of losing one's mate does not in itself provoke jealousy. Neither does the loss of a mate. A husband suffering intensely because his wife has left him for another man may rationalize his emotions by insisting that he cannot live without her. The fallacy of this conviction would immediately become apparent if he were asked how he would feel if she were dead. He would then admit that alternative to be terrible, and yet . . . Here he might stop and discover that it is a peculiar kind of love which makes him actually prefer her death to her living with someone else.

Infidelity often is just a bugaboo. Every look one's husband casts may foretell potential fatal complications. Slight tendencies to infidelity are certainly not less frequent or more dangerous than a common cold. It can lead to fatal pneumonia, but generally does not. Putting a person to bed at the first sniffle is as foolish as letting him go out in the rain when his temperature rises. A simple cold needs proper care; either neglect or overanxiety can be harmful. The first signs of undue extra-marital interests indicate disorder. Neglect or overzealousness can complicate the ailment. A clever and understanding mate will find many subtle ways of drawing an adventuring partner back without oppressing his feeling of freedom and independence. Jealousy is neither helpful nor necessary.

If fear of loss and fear of infidelity do not necessarily entail jealousy, what then are its causes? In order to understand any human emotion we must discover its actual accomplishments and hence its purposes. Jealousy never prevents loss or infidelity. This fact alone proves convincingly that it is psychologically not concerned with either. But what is actually achieved by jealousy?

THE PURPOSE OF JEALOUSY

Since our emotions impress us strongly and convincingly that we are right and the other one wrong, we find it difficult to accept a psychological interpretation of our own jealousy. Jealousy may have different meanings; all depends upon the purpose for which jealousy is used. Disturbing emotions are only found in support of socially disturbing behavior. Such behavior is generally directed toward one of the following four directions:

> Excuse for shortcomings
> Attracting attention

Gaining power
Vengeance

EXCUSE FOR SHORTCOMINGS

Doubt in oneself is an essential factor. As long as we do not doubt our own adequacy, our influence and our attraction, we never can be jealous. The most trying situation will not provoke suspicion and fear in a courageous person sure of his ability to overcome the danger. We become jealous when we question whether we, ourselves, give enough. We become afraid that someone else may offer more —we become jealous, provoking quarrels and disappointment, which in turn serve to make us more uncertain of our position in the other one's life; and this increased feeling of inadequacy intensifies our provocative jealousy. In this vicious circle, jealousy is the link which enables us to act hostilely and aggressively, although we should know better. With common sense, we could recognize that we must make up for our shortcomings. Our lack of courage forbids this admission. As we fear we are incapable of doing better, we need emotion for other compensation. And, paradoxically, jealousy hinders us from being good when we know that we are not good enough.

The feeling of inadequacy can refer to one's personal worth in general, or to one's sufficiency for husband or wife, or finally, to one's status among one's own sex. The question of personal worth preoccupies individuals who from childhood have had the tendency to disbelieve their own value. Many odd ways are sought to hide this lack of faith. In one it may be a desire for perfection, and no merit, no talent, no admiration prevents such a person from feel-

132

ing neglected. Security is pursued, but never attained. Since nothing but death is certain, the pursuit of security is hopeless. The sense of insecurity becomes a torture and demands compensations. Jealousy acts as justification for demands which common sense could not allow. The person who looks for a guarantee of security, as far as his mate is concerned, is constantly jealous, regardless of what he gets.

Temporary jealousy often arises at the very moment when we become aware of our shortcomings in regard to marital obligation. The desire to accuse is often an attempt to avoid accusation. This psychological mechanism leads to peculiar situations. Very often a breach of faithfulness is immediately followed by a spell of jealousy. The following story is not unique.

A young woman lived in a very unsatisfactory marriage. She cared little for her husband, whose qualities and behavior she despised. So she finally decided to get a divorce. Before breaking up completely, however, she went on a vacation to see how the temporary separation would affect them both. She had a grand time, felt carefree and relaxed, and without any deep interest began an affair with a young man. When she returned home, her husband, as she had expected, was not at the railroad station to welcome her. But she was hurt, upset, and for the first time became jealous. She imagined him with another woman, neglecting her badly. This new feeling did not change her attitude toward him and they soon were divorced, but this strange incident puzzled her. For a moment, she suspected that she might love him unknowingly, but it was not true, and she went on with the divorce proceedings. What had actually happened was that for the first time she became uncertain of whether she had behaved correctly in her relationship with him, whether she had fulfilled her obligation as wife and woman. Without this doubt in herself, she would not have hoped that her husband, never considerate before and now almost es-

133

tranged, would meet her at the train; and without jealousy, she would not have granted herself any right to demand anything from him after she had failed.

One frequent element in jealousy is competition with the same sex. Our relationship with a person of the opposite sex is very much colored by our attitude toward our own. Women whose life centers very much around men and who therefore regard every other woman as their mortal enemy may think of their own husband as a poor dupe endangered by all the scheming cats. The competition between men is more concerned with business and work, and women play a minor, although not at all negligible, role. Men who doubt their masculinity, who envy other males by regarding them as "real men" such as they themselves never were and never will be, are inclined to be sensitive to the favors which their wives grant other men. The third party often attracts much more interest and evokes more emotions than the wife whose unfaithfulness seemed to be the reason for all the upheaval. Jealousy being not at all focused on her, hostile acts, backed by corresponding feelings, are directed not primarily against her, but against the competitor who is feared to be actually or potentially superior.

As an expression of mere discouragement, whether in the competition with one's mate or with someone of one's own sex, jealousy serves as an excuse for the intensification of warfare and for acts of aggression or impoliteness which a decent, loving person otherwise would never permit himself. The culprit, who commits these acts, shifts the blame for them to his victim.

134

*ATTRACTING ATTENTION AND GAINING
POWER*

The feeling of inadequacy and inferiority stimulates a striving for compensation. The method easiest and closest at hand is to attempt to gain attention. People who are unsure whether they are sufficiently loved and appreciated continuously demand signs of devotion. Jealousy serves their purpose well. Every outside interest which demands time and attention from the mate appears as dangerous— every attention paid another person as infringing on their own rights of property. This continuous request for attention leads frequently to tyranny, especially if the original demands for unlimited attention are not fully gratified. The ensuing feeling of being neglected leads to intensified claims. Under the pretext of love and devotion, the jealous person guards every step of the mate. And God save both if the mate supervised does not attend strictly to the rules imposed! If unwilling to accept the responsibility for outbursts of pain, suffering, and violence, he had better submit carefully to the demands of his jealous mate. The latter, of course, is completely "innocent," driven by emotions which are stronger than the "best intentions"; and above all, his actual, unquestionable anguish "exonerates" any misbehavior.

Mrs. O. had grown up as an only girl among several brothers. She was always the center of attention and managed to keep this position. When she got married, she suffered a great deal from her feeling of jealousy, which she recognized as being unjustified. She asked her husband time and again about his previous experiences with women, despite the fact—or perhaps because of it?—that he assured her each time how much more

135

attractive she was and that he loved her more than he had ever loved anyone else. She still doubted her ability to compare favorably with the physical beauty of other women. She made no secret of her jealousy and spent many hours in rather tortuous discussions with her husband. With her jealousy she kept control of every one of his movements. Whenever she felt neglected she called on him at his office, trying to find out whether he was with another woman. Under the pressure of her jealousy, she prevented him from leaving her alone, disregarding many of his professional and social obligations which would keep him away from her. Once, when her efforts to keep him home failed, she used jealousy as a weapon against him by immediately arranging a date with another man, to make him jealous too. She relied upon jealousy in either form, suffering from it or provoking it.

SEEKING VENGEANCE

If this intensified warfare, with tyranny and outbursts of complaint, does not guarantee position and power—and it never does, because it only increases opposition and rebellion in the opponent—then the last phase of open hostility is reached. The jealousy is employed as a terrible weapon of vengeance. Ingeniously, the jealous person detects the spot where the "beloved" enemy can be hurt most. Under the protection of rage, the most outrageous accusations are voiced, the most cutting remarks shrewdly assault the victim's dignity and self-respect, so that what remains is a quivering bundle of crushed despair, something without human dignity.

INDUCING JEALOUSY IN THE MATE

Not seldom do we ourselves provoke jealousy without realizing it. Keeping our mate in suspense by not committing ourselves is likely to produce a deep feeling of insecurity and inadequacy. Sometimes people induce jealousy in the partner to gain or regain interest and attention. Sometimes we provoke jealousy in order to have a reason for quarreling or for any other purpose not admitted to ourselves.

One of my students once complained bitterly about the jealousy of his wife. For the past few months they had quarreled daily. She accused him of spending his time with other women or paying too much attention to his family and neglecting her. A brief analysis of the situation and especially of the conditions under which these quarrels had started revealed an amazing fact. He had found himself confronted with a difficult and decisive examination. At this moment his wife's jealousy had started. Was this only coincidental? Definitely not. Without being aware of what he did he actually had changed his behavior toward her in such a way that she couldn't help becoming suspicious. While he had previously been a very considerate and attentive husband, he was now actually neglecting her. He came home later than he had promised, showed no interest in her problems, was over-sensitive and aggressive. No wonder she suspected another woman. And he, instead of dispelling her suspicions, had increased them by arguing and by scolding her, without mentioning his real troubles.

This situation could be regarded as a mere misunderstanding between husband and wife; but it was more. By repeatedly complaining that his wife's jealousy made it impossible to study and concentrate, he plainly revealed how conveniently this jealousy had occurred. It excused his expected shortcomings and soothed his vanity. Anyone unfamiliar with the trickery of the human mind will consider it impossible that he had purposely, although unconsciously, made his wife jealous. The explanation may sound fanciful, but the development showed how correct it was. Shortly after it had been explained to him that he had unwittingly stirred up quarrels and dissension in order to excuse his assumed inadequacy, the home situation changed. After he became aware of his secret plans, it was impossible to continue them. Without any specific action or effort on his

137

side, his wife stopped being jealous. He himself was amazed at the changes in his home after he overcame his fears of the examination and stopped looking for excuses.

UNDERSTANDING AND HELPING A JEALOUS MATE

It is necessary to understand the psychology of a jealous person; otherwise we remain blind to the actual causes. Psychological information must be handled very carefully, however, if worse disaster is to be avoided. Let us stop for a moment to consider the value of the preceding paragraphs. For the jealous person himself they are of scarcely any use, because he cannot see himself clearly when he is succumbing to emotions. Anyone confronted with a jealous person will not find it difficult to recognize the psychological factors. But what use will he make of them? That is the decisive point for any psychological information. We must realize that psychology, like any other human device, can be used to good or bad purposes. It can be used as a most powerful weapon of destruction—or it can be the basis for sympathy and understanding. If the victim of a jealous person refers to scientific discovery in pointing out to his adversary that he uses his emotions only to get attention or to tyrannize, the result will be far from beneficial. It will only infuriate the more and aggravate the unhappy relationship. Psychological insight can be used properly only by avoiding carefully any verbal expression of what one knows, using instead the knowledge for adequate behavior and helpful action.

Can we help a mate who is jealous? What can a husband who has a jealous wife do? Most people who experience this predicament will deny that anything can be done. They may point out that the other person is not susceptible to "reason." They do not know that they mean by reason an utterly futile attempt to persuade. Because they resort to wrong methods, they consider the condition incurable.

Let us imagine a rather common situation. The husband, coming home in the evening, finds his wife in sullen silence. She does not respond to his greeting. There is tension in the air. "What is the matter with you?" Still she does not speak. Obviously she is angry. He, too, becomes angry and demands some explanation. Finally she bursts out, "You can go back to your girl friend. Why trouble to come home at all?"

What does the husband in such a situation generally do? If he is kind and considerate, he may attempt to talk her out of it, trying to convince her that she is wrong. Very soon he will make the typical mistake of apologizing for his tardiness. She will not believe him, no matter what he says. He himself will get more excited and angry. (People talk too much—in anger, in bitterness. Talk can bring people together when they are in a friendly mood; but when they fight and are angry, words are as bad as slashes and whips and hurt more than any physical assault.)

This is the usual procedure in a jealous love quarrel: The accused tries to exonerate himself. We all believe so much in logic and understand so little of psychology! Instead of acting psychologically, we try to talk logically.

Logic is far from being as effective as we are inclined to believe. We can be entirely right, but we are wrong when we try to explain that we are right. We forget to take into consideration whether or not the circumstances are conducive to logical reasoning. It is unimportant whether we

139

are right or wrong, and it is definitely insufficient to be right. Even if we are wrong, we may succeed if we act right psychologically. But we will never succeed if we are logically right and act wrong psychologically. The attitude of our opponent, backed by strong emotions, will never be changed by arguments, logical or not. For every clever argument we may use, the other person has three better ones. The outcome can be only mutual indignation and anger—a quarrel to the bitter end until both have become exhausted and repentant, having punished each other to the utmost.

Another mistake is characteristic in dealing with a jealous person. Because we do not understand what is going on in his mind, we do not realize what causes his actual suffering; we recognize only the injustice done to us. We feel accused without reason, hurt without justification. Our own inadequacy in the precarious situation makes us angry. As we do not know what to do, we become hostile and fight too. Instead of one person being wrong, now there are two.

Often enough jealous feelings can be assuaged in a clever and subtle way—if we are sure of ourselves, if we refrain from regarding ourselves as being humiliated and abused. A little smile, a kind expression of patience, a kiss full of tenderness, a word of sincere affection may work wonders. We may find a pleasant distraction, soothing the excitement, if we can wait a little. Scolding and arguing never will promote essential relaxation. Only after the atmosphere has cleared and tension is gone is there opportunity for effective help.

And the jealous person needs our help. Telling him that he is wrong is superfluous. Everyone knows the wrongness of yielding to jealousy. Actually, he is far less wrong than it seems from a logical point of view. But since he does not understand himself he expresses himself wrongly. The accusations are wrong, logically. But the *feeling* of being inadequate or neglected is not false. It is a psychological fact. The sympathetic mate can do a great deal toward encouraging and providing a certain sense of security. The mother-in-law or the imaginary other man or woman is only incidental. Keeping up an argument about them is beside the point. But assurances of one's love and affection reach the roots of the disturbance. Signs of appreciation and esteem may avert any inclination toward jealousy. Letting the other person know how much he is needed may help him to overcome his feeling of inadequacy.

Another frequent mistake must be avoided. While we reproach and quarrel, resent and scorn, we generally succumb to the demands of the jealous person. We try to appease by giving in. We promise not to see the other man or woman any more, or to visit mother less frequently. But this brings no solution. It stimulates the conviction that if we are scolded enough, we will yield. Besides that, it does not produce a good conscience in the accuser. Although jealousy triumphs, the triumphant partner realizes the discomfort he has caused, and each victory only increases the fear of unavoidable final defeat. These few points should be remembered whenever you are dealing with a jealous person: don't excuse yourself, and don't try to reason or to convince; but do not give in either. Be firm, and do what you think is right. Surrender will help as little as fighting. But give the partner what he actually needs—affection and devotion.

JEALOUSY AS A PSYCHIATRIC PROBLEM

From the psychiatric point of view, it is generally most difficult to cure deeply disturbed persons of their jealousy. If they come for help at all, they want assistance—against their mates. They demonstrate with all their intellectual power the injustice and unfairness of their mates. They are seldom ready to be informed about themselves. They want a change in the behavior of the partner, not of themselves. Therapeutic help and influence can be effective only if the jealous person is sincere in his desire to be helped.

One way to cure a jealous person is to demonstrate to him convincingly what he wants. Calling his emotion and his behavior foolish and senseless makes no impression. Such remarks or reproaches miss the point entirely. First, his feeling is real. It might have no sense, but it exists and hurts. Further, the jealous person himself might agree and admit that his jealousy is unreasonable. But does that help? On the contrary, it only clouds the real issue. No one has meaningless emotions; one may be just unaware of their meaning.

The therapy of jealousy, therefore, is a problem of general psychotherapy. The underlying causes of the disturbance must be explored first, and the patient must be helped in understanding himself, not only in regard to his present conflicts, but in his whole outlook on life, in his life style. This understanding and insight, however, is not sufficient, and not even significant, unless it leads to a change, to a correction of faulty concepts and approaches, to a reorientation in regard to social position and social participation. Unjustified, although understandable, inferiority feelings

142

must be eliminated; the deficiency in the social interest of the patient, based on his experiences and erroneous interpretations during childhood, must be overcome. In this way the patient develops new courage and self-confidence for handling his social problems more effectively and correctly.

Very disturbed persons may resist any effort to treat them, although they may pretend to seek help. The jealousy of a chronic alcoholic cannot be treated without freeing the patient first of his addiction. Jealousy is sometimes a symptom of a more severe mental disorder, classified as a paranoiac state; sometimes it is an obsessive idea belonging in the group of severe neuroses. In these cases the prognosis of the treatment is not good.

OVERCOMING OUR OWN JEALOUSY

For the average person it is most important to know what one can do for one's own adjustment if one suffers from the tendency to be jealous. Insight into our own tendencies can help a great deal. Undoubtedly, when our own emotions are involved, insight is difficult and change even more so. As soon as we excuse our behavior on the basis of our feelings and emotions, we exclude reason as an efficient factor. Emotions fortify attitudes so strongly that no other influence is likely to succeed. That is why it is so difficult to overcome jealousy in ourselves.

Why do we abandon reason, the exercise of which would inhibit emotions? Partly because it is characteristic of all emotions to appear and disappear without apparent reason and logic. We are therefore convinced that we can hardly influence them, let alone change them by reasoning with

143

ourselves. The belief that emotions are uncontrollable—that they are stronger than reason—is a part of our culture that dates back thousands of years. It is not true that flesh is weaker than spirit. Flesh cannot do anything that the spirit will not allow. Behind strong unreasonable feelings lie concrete and very practical intentions. It is possible to overcome emotions, if we are courageous enough to admit their significance and implications—their tendencies and objectives.

If we are jealous, it is not sufficient to admit that we have behaved wrongly; we can make such an admission and still feel that our intentions were good. Real insight demands scrutiny of our actual intentions. Do we want to gain more attention? Do we want to exert pressure and power? Do we intend to hurt, or to excuse our failure in marriage? Only after we accept full responsibility for our intentions and thereby also for our emotions can we help ourselves. The woman who is jealous of her husband's visiting his mother instead of coming home is not concerned with her mother-in-law, nor even with her husband; but with herself, her position, her value. By becoming jealous she tries to demonstrate to him that he cannot neglect her, that he is not permitted to care for anyone more than for her; and if he does not pay attention to her in the way she wishes, then he must devote his time and energy to her in quarrels. And if he does not conform with her desires, he must suffer.

The most effective way to overcome emotions of antagonism is to realize the purpose for which we create and maintain them. If we understand and sincerely admit our aims to ourselves, we discover how truly we are masters of our emotions, for good or for bad. This insight is rather difficult to achieve. We are ready to admit the psychological factors which apparently have caused our emotions; doubt of oneself and others, feelings of inadequacy, competition with the same sex—these are easily recognized. But this knowledge helps very little as long as we accept these facts as final. "That's true, but what can I do?" Insight into our aims pertains to entirely different psychological dynamics. The realization that we create jealousy in order to dominate weakens the emotion, so that it can no longer be used as an adequate excuse for our actions.

IMPROVEMENT STARTS WITH ONESELF

Jealousy starts the vicious circle. When it enters the marital relationship, the typical conflict situation arises: instead of realizing that the jealousy of one spouse is a common problem of both of them, each one turns against the other and wants him to solve the conflict. Each is willing to cooperate, if only the other one would not make it so difficult. Yet as long as each demands that the other change first, there is no hope for improvement. It becomes only a struggle for superiority, a contest as to who is to give in first. And neither will. So both become hopeless and the decrease of their optimism intensifies their aggressiveness and convinces both that nothing can be salvaged but each one's own prestige. Thus they are deadlocked in a struggle where they pay with misery for a conquest which they can enjoy only for a few minutes—until they meet the next defeat. They remain unaware of how much they actually could do to solve their problem.

One of the fundamental prerequisites to a solution is the recognition that the only point at which either one can start is with himself. No other basis for successful and effective action can be found. Confronted with any marital problem, the only question which leads to a constructive solution is, "What can *I* do?" By sincere effort to discover what each can himself contribute, the gate can open to a way out of even the most disturbing and apparently hopeless predicament. No situation can be so desperate as to offer no possibility of betterment. Finding the best possible answer cannot always eliminate discomfort and distress, but it generally leads to a less complicated situation and finally to a satisfactory solution which at first may have seemed impossible. Many demand a perfect solution for a problem not yet ripe for any satisfactory conclusion. They forget that there is still the way of improvement. Slow as it may be, it usually is the only way leading toward cooperation and satisfaction.

These remarks pertain to all marital problems. We have chosen jealousy only as one example, illustrating the nature of any friction. To conclude our discussion with some practical suggestions which are applicable to jealousy as much as to any other discord: Although each person must start by himself, more assistance can be expected from the one who suffers less at a given moment. At the start of a love quarrel, the jealous person probably is the most miserable one—therefore, the other has his chance before he himself becomes equally miserable. What can one do?

First, one should try to understand the predicament of the mate. Why is he jealous? And what did one do, unintentionally, to add to this jealousy? Did the wife fail to give the husband sufficient signs of her devotion, or did she perhaps provoke a sense of insecurity in him? Did she perhaps, in her vanity, convince him that he was not good enough? After somehow making good this failure of hers, which has contributed to the present tension, she may proceed to offer encouragement and comfort, avoiding a relapse into the pre-existing antagonism, fully aware that he needs her help now—not afterward. And in helping him, she helps herself, now and afterward.

How can we prevent ourselves from becoming jealous? If we are truly conscientious and eager to maintain marital peace and harmony, we should become alert to any sign of hostility in ourselves. (It is characteristic of our present-day insecurity that we are very sensitive to the slightest indication of hostility—but only on the part of other people toward us.) Any hostile emotion we feel should be a warning. What is going on within us? Do we detect a fatal drop in self-confidence, an overshadowing pessimism gnawing at our courage? Then danger and destruction lie ahead. Let us not be fooled: the source of our indignation seems to be outside, but it is within ourselves. It is time now to consider where we are going. Why do we doubt ourselves? Why don't we look for a way up instead of striking down? We need emotions, but emotions of enthusiasm, of hope, of eagerness, of optimism and sympathy. Let us be wary of any hostility we feel.

Finding a better psychological approach to ourselves, we prepare the way for improvement. The conflict situation is only a symptom. We cannot cure it without attacking the basic underlying deterioration. We cannot expect to change our emotions without changing somewhat our attitudes toward life—our conceptions of ourselves, the methods which we employ. Each conflict is a test of our human

147

fellowship, of our social interest. If we get discouraged, if we become hostile and lose our sense of belonging, conflicts may lead to disaster. Otherwise, conflicts may stimulate progress and evolution, increasing our wisdom and our experience, producing an improvement in our technique of living and raising our self-confidence. Every conflict situation handled adequately is a step forward. It reveals the shortcomings in our upbringing, the limitations of our socialization. Only timid people run away from friction; for the courageous, problems exist in order to be solved. Let us accept this challenge to improve. Let us learn to demand less and to live better, more happily, together.

VII.

MARITAL PROBLEMS AND CONFLICTS

THE NATURE OF HUMAN PROBLEMS

COUNTLESS are the problems which we have to meet in living together. Our whole lifetime is given over to overcoming obstacles. Marriage is of definite advantage, for it brings together two people for mutual help in the struggle for existence. But though marriage helps us to meet the tasks of life—it is also a task which must be met. In matrimony we encounter not only the general problems of life, but the special problems arising in marriage. We may consider problems as a test of our capacity to solve them. Our marital problems are a test of our ability to live closely together with another human being.

These considerations suggest that every problem is related to various levels of our personality and our life. It is on the superficial level that the actual content of a problem appears first. We are aware of uneasiness. This subjective feeling of calamity seems to be caused entirely by a definite concrete situation. Economic, social, professional, or sexual conflicts seem to demand special efforts. If these

149

efforts do not resolve the problem, disappointment and discontent follow. Formerly assistance and advice were limited to specific regulations which had to be observed in order to maintain cooperation and harmony in life or marriage. The suggestions offered were technical, recommending specific procedures to be followed to meet specific evident circumstances. Written laws directed personal conduct.

The modern psychologist seeks behind any concrete problem a structure totally different from the evident problem itself, which can be regarded as merely a symptom. Each problem is related to the entirety of a given life situation, which is established by all forces converging on us from the outside and meeting our personal attitude deriving from our past—our style of life, our training, our preparation.

Any constructive discussion of the problems causing discontent and friction must disclose psychological errors which have provoked the problems or are hindering their satisfactory solution. Although it seems to us that our encounter with life results in real and concrete clashes which hurt, insult, and sometimes even kill, in reality the conflict is only within ourselves. The question, whether reality exists at all, or only in our conception of it, remained a mere philosophical issue—and a very confused and confusing one—until physicists revealed the "spiritual nature" of matter, discovering that any concrete substance, tangible as it is, consists entirely of abstract and utterly immaterial waves. The chair on which one sits is real, it consists of wood or metal. One might expect to find the same material no matter how far one analyzes the constituents of the chair, but that is wrong. If one goes far enough, one finds particles which consist only of electrons, neutrons, and other smallest bodies which, however, are actually only waves without what we generally consider substance. The speed and number of waves alone determine the material, wood or metal, the consistency, whether solid, liquid, or gaseous, and the color. We are living in an entirely different world when we look behind the surface of the "real thing." Great is the similarity between the conception and approach of modern physical science and psychology.[1] The analysis of concrete problems discloses a similar fundamental difference between the appearance of a problem and the forces constituting it. Each problem is the expression of personal and social forces beneath the surface. Solution of conflicts demands an understanding of the underlying facts, of conditions and personalities involved.

THE SUBJECTIVITY OF FACTS

As long as life goes on, forces will oppose each other, interests will clash, demands will conflict. Life always will be succumbing to death, and growth will always try to survive destruction. That is true for life as a whole, as well as for any part of it. It is as true for the cell as for the organism; for the unit of the family as well as for the nation and the world. Clash and collision do not necessarily mean suffering. Even death is rarely painful. Real mishaps are responsible for only a minor amount of our grief and unhappiness. It is hard to believe, but true, that death, disease,

[1] A. S. Eddington says in regard to the new concepts of physics about matter: "It is difficult for the matter-of-fact physicist to accept the view that the substratum of everything is of mental character. But . . . mind is the first and most direct thing in our experience, and all else is remote inference." *The Nature of the Physical World.* The Macmillan Company, New York, 1928.

151

war, and poverty cause only a small part of the misery which plagues mankind today. The ability of human nature to adjust itself to the most atrocious conditions is amazing. Our suffering takes place within ourselves. It comes from our attitudes toward facts, it lies in our minds. This does not mean that we dare be oblivious to the conditions of life; on the contrary, we recognize now more than ever the interrelationship between facts and mind. We know the human mind creates facts and conditions and is itself stimulated by conditions and experiences. There is a constant interaction between an individual and his environment. But whether any situation is pleasant or unpleasant depends only to a limited degree upon the situation itself. Our attitude spells acceptance or rejection—and only rejection is connected with unpleasant sensations.

Our attitude determines the meaning of facts. Facts in themselves, life in itself, are neither good nor bad—pleasant nor unpleasant. What we make of them counts. Almost everything contains all possibilities; even death or pain may be acceptable and welcome. Pain as a sign of healing or of progress (giving birth, or as first sign of recovery in paralysis) may be highly pleasant. Good may stem from anything, as may evil. A given circumstance may destroy or it may stimulate. Our own determination, our preconceived opinion directs our view to the beautiful or the ugly and enables us to find help or disaster. Our "biased apperception" turns reality into fiction: we see what we like to see, we find what we expect to find. We learn by experience only to a limited degree, because we generally "make" our experiences; that is, arrange them—arrange them and definitely interpret them as we choose.

152

This "idealistic" interpretation of life is accused of neglecting any conflict produced by conditions outside ourselves. According to our everyday experiences, our life seems to be determined by strong environing forces, in comparison to which our own individual strength appears puny. Hereditary or hygienic conditions, economic security or unemployment, war or prosperity have decisive influence on the course of our life. A group of people, persecuted and suppressed, can scarcely include or beget happy individuals, and starved people can rarely be optimistic. Are social forces not more important than personal attitudes?

Contradictory points of view are responsible for many misunderstandings in personal relationships, in research, in counseling. Materialism and idealism represent different aspects of life. For a long time economic and sociological approaches to human problems were exclusively materialistic; religious and philosophic conceptions by contrast were more or less idealistic. Today, however, we are moving toward an integrated conception of life. We find in psychology as well as in sociology both mechanistic and idealistic tendencies. Behaviorists, for instance, recognize only the tangible influences upon the individual, while semanticists regard personal interpretations and conceptions as decisive factors. It seems difficult to unite both points of view. In our endeavor to combine these two aspects, both seeming true and yet each contradicting the other, we receive assistance from modern physical science. Physicists point out that what we call causality is the law of the great number, which is better called "statistical probability"—while the single particle seems to be undetermined and unpredictable in its movement and speed. Applied to human

153

problems, this notion of causality has interesting consequences.

Sociological factors are material influences which determine the fate of the *masses*. Such influences are decisive only for a great number, but not for the individual. The number of people in the United States who are unemployed depends on economic and social conditions, the influence of which is strictly deterministic. Any improvement of these conditions produces an increase of employment, and any deterioration a corresponding decrease. This relationship is deterministic. But whether you and I are unemployed is determined neither by economic and social conditions nor by the number of unemployed. It is up to us how we meet the necessity of earning a living. If we try harder and more efficiently, we may get a job—although at the expense of someone else, who may be fired,[2] or we may create a job.

This is the idealistic approach to a problem contrasted to causalistic determinism. Both approaches have a definite value, if we distinguish clearly that the first should be employed in considering individual problems, and the second in judging general conditions. The percentage of persons who commit suicide in a given community remains amazingly constant from year to year, and is related to economic conditions (the price of grain, for instance) or to social and political circumstances which alone cause increase or decrease in the number. During war and revolution the number of suicides generally decreases. But whether an *individual* commits suicide or not is entirely independent of the price of grain, or the war situation.

[2] This should not be interpreted, of course, as being a solution to the problem of unemployment!

Although exposed to all general influences, his actions are not fully determined by them, nor has any other factor decisive, unalterable power over him. The individual is free to make his plans and to act accordingly. His own attitude, formed on the spur of the moment, but on the basis of and in agreement with his personal style of life, decides which steps he will take and in which direction he will move.

THE BACKGROUND OF MARITAL CONFLICTS

All marital problems have the general social background of our times. This is the reason why, as we have already mentioned, the problems of thousands of men and women are alike. Each example of conflict and friction between a husband and wife reflects the influence of the general problems which today confront mankind. Economic insecurity; the helplessness which so many feel in regard to social, political, and economic issues of our times; the lack of stability, produced by profound changes of values and morals; the disintegration of our society into small units, each one looking out for its own interest; the deep suspicion against each other, produced by the prevalent competition and rivalry; and most of all, the contest for prestige between men and women—these are the elements which give to otherwise trivial and insignificant disputes depth and meaning. Knowing these facts, however, helps little in overcoming the predicaments of husbands and wives. To be useful, knowledge must be applicable. Unfortunately, technical advice alone is of limited value, also, because the personal attitude is the most important motive behind the scenes.

155

Understanding of one's self and one's partner, insight into the relevant aspects of human nature, will probably prove the most efficient assistance which man can find in his difficult task of meeting life and being married.

THE PROBLEM OF SEXUAL INCOMPATIBILITY

In discussing what are commonly regarded as stumbling blocks to happiness, let us keep our eyes open for the deep underlying human conflicts and needs. Sexual compatibility is considered one of the fundamentals of marital understanding, since marriage is the legal institution providing for sexual gratification. Strangely enough, mutual sexual satisfaction is more the exception than the rule in our present-day marriages. Since the high frequency of sexual dissatisfaction became apparent, a host of books have been written to improve marital sex relationships. Much has been written about the differences in the masculine and feminine sex rhythm, and how to overcome the obstacles thus created. People have craved this kind of literature, hoping to receive an answer to their hunger for satisfying experiences. Many couples may have found some comfort from these books. Yet I still wonder whether their new lease on sexual happiness was derived from the technical advice or from the new attitude of a disillusioned couple united again by a mutual curiosity and the adventure of sharing a common task. It is possible that this sharing might bring about a deeper, more lasting unity of purpose and interest than that established by the wedding; but a new technique alone cannot have permanent effects or save a deteriorating union.

156

The phrase "sexual incompatibility" is too readily used and generally misused as an excuse to conceal rejection. Unquestionably each individual is sexually more attracted by certain types of the other sex than by others. Previous experiences and personal inclinations result in individual preferences. Although it happens, however rarely, that a person feels attracted to one type alone, such preference can be of importance only during the process of courting. After the wedding other factors rule the sexual relationship. The most favored "type" may soon lose all attraction. We have mentioned a case in which the husband rediscovered his wife sexually after he had been convinced that she could never stimulate him again. Lack of sexual interest in general, failing sexual stimulation, diversity of sexual demands, inadequate sexual procedure, impotence and frigidity, sexual repulsiveness or aversion, these are not the causes of any so-called sexual incompatibility but the consequence of personal conflicts. They reflect antagonistic attitudes between husband and wife; these attitudes influence their sexual behavior. Without any technical instruction—which nevertheless unquestionably has its merit—two people who love each other sincerely can discover each other sexually and can remain sexually attracted.

Materialists overrate the importance of sexual constitution and of full gratification. They believe in sexual predestination and in the physical exhaustion of desire. Let us consider the facts. Very frequently the wedding night is the first great disappointment, and only too often marks the beginning of marital disillusionment and unhappiness. Bride and groom cannot find mutual satisfaction, nor later on do they learn to understand each other better. Their sexual constitution is too different, they explain. Or they find themselves swept by their passion, burning in ecstasy and after a short while the flame subsides. Their desire sated, they look for new sex stimulations, new ventures, new experiences. Even in less extreme cases, such people may believe that stimulation cannot survive the daily routine; that new experiences are necessary to keep the desire burning—that monotony kills pleasure. Millions of people believe in innate sexual compatibility and natural dissipation of desire, because their experiences seem to corroborate such belief, and they are unable to look more deeply into these experiences.

GRATIFICATION REQUIRES MUTUAL ADJUSTMENT

When two people enter a sexual relationship, each brings into the union his personality, a host of past experiences—and, of course, his physical constitution, too. It must be an extraordinary coincidence if they really match perfectly. Lovemaking is an art, the perfection of which has to be developed through training, like any other art. The better artists they are, the better they immediately fit together. But even if they do not know the art at all, and even though they may differ in their initial attitudes, they can learn together. Every sex relationship is a process of mutual adjustment, if it goes beyond the first act of passionate release.

Let us state first some of the differences which two lovers meet in each other: each can be passive or active, demanding or submissive, leading or following. Each may be aggressive or patient, ruthless or sensitive, self-centered or

158

considerate. All these qualities are expressed in sexual behavior. In some traits or habits there might be a natural agreement, a mutual harmony. May we ever expect it in all personal traits and habits? How little does the pair know of each other before they fuse so closely—and, therefore, how easily are they disappointed! Further, they meet in each other their whole individual pasts. What they have experienced, what they have liked, what they have dreamed—it all emerges in the one moment of unification. Hundreds of people meet in the one couple.

But lovers do not realize their own unseen participants—and they are disappointed if the whole crowd of people do not match. All the affections which were given and received, all emotions toward the beloved ones, images of father or mother, brother or sister, of boy friends or girl friends—they all converge in the person with whom we merge in love. We do not experience a real person, but at first a symbol of whatever we have loved, whatever we have expected. Even if the circumstances are favorable and the mate can live up to every demand, we sooner or later awaken from the dream. Then we must learn to recognize our partner and to love the person. But if we love him for what he stands for in our mind, we become disappointed, and withdraw. Our love can persist only if the new experience is strong enough to conquer the past and to open a new chapter in our demands and expectations. If the mates fail to make this necessary mutual adjustment, sexual disappointment and increasing disharmony result.

Mr. and Mrs. A. consulted me in regard to their unsatisfactory sexual life. They were devoted to each other. A fine spirit of cooperation helped them to understand each other and to agree generally in solving their mutual life problems; but sexually they had drifted completely apart, and were now at the point where they could not enjoy each other at all. The decisive factor in their disappointment seemed to be the difference in their emotional training. Mrs. A., it happened, was an only child of a very affectionate mother, and had grown up in an atmosphere of tenderness and openly expressed devotion. Mr. A., however, had left his family when he was thirteen years old, had supported himself from that time on, and had spent his youth as a sailor. When he finally desired to settle down, to have a home and family of his own, Mrs. A. impressed him with her motherly devotion, and he fell in love with her. She loved him, because he was self-sufficient, a strong man who gave promise of protection and stability. Both were right in their expectation, but missed the grade on one point. She could not indulge in mere tender fondling with him without arousing his sexual desire. He rejected her demand just to be close to him, to be kissed and caressed, and she resented his brutal overpowering of her. During the years the mutual resentment grew stronger and stronger until he became impotent and completely lost any sexual desire, because he felt her painful and reluctant submission. Both failed to learn to love what the other one liked; each felt cheated in his own "justified" demands. Both wanted to receive satisfaction and not to give it.

ATTITUDES MORE IMPORTANT THAN TECHNIQUES

This striving for being gratified is unfortunately very common, and is the source of much friction and disappointment. Few recognize the sexual satisfaction which lies in satisfying. Not that they do not intend to satisfy, but they do not live in each other—only in themselves. What matters is their own feeling, their own ability, their own being hurt or rejected. They do not get away from themselves. Gratifying love means experiencing and feeling the other lover, unreservedly, unconditionally. As soon as one experiences

160

a feeling of demand, the mind withdraws from the other and centers around one's self.

The same is true if the feeling of obligation or of threat to one's prestige develops. Although one seems to be interested in fulfilling his duty, this feeling of obligation—this interest in whether one will be capable or not—is incompatible with fully sensing the partner. Any interest beside mutual enjoyment and gratification distracts and kills the emotion. Impotence and frigidity are the consequences of emotional withdrawal. They are neurotic mechanisms and conceal the true intentions, as any neurotic symptoms do. While one seems consciously concerned with gratifying and gratification, one is actually more interested in one's own prestige or failure and other problems of defense. It is resentment toward their feminine role that makes many women hesitant to play their feminine part in the communion, and this resentment creates frigidity. Often women are not even aware that they are frigid, for they love their husbands and even feel sexually stimulated. But they lack the final emotional climax which indicates complete surrender. Others vainly expect certain stimulation because they don't realize that they themselves hinder the development of their emotions to full capacity. Masculine impotency is similar. Impotence means either a desire to keep aloof, to keep distance, or it reflects a profound doubt of being a "real man." Lack of sexual stimulation or insufficient depth of emotion always mean withholding and desire for distance, often originated by marital discontent and disagreement in other spheres of life.

It is necessary to consider the physiological difference between masculine and feminine rhythm of sexual sensations, which has been discussed so much recently. What is generally overlooked is the fact that men and women must under any circumstances adjust themselves to each other, because no two persons have the same training. The danger in the sexual relationship is the tendency to make demands upon each other. He or she *should* act and respond differently, slowly or more quickly, gently or violently, adding or omitting certain actions. Unquestionably we educate each other, but never by demanding. A demand only irritates and creates discord and opposition.

If mutual gratification is not obtained automatically, one must start the process of adjustment by oneself. Women are more easily disappointed than men. It is a question whether their retarded reaction is of physiological origin or an expression of their general hesitant attitude toward sexual fulfillment, apparently demanded by social convention. This training of passivity makes women more inclined to demand and to be disappointed, expecting solutions from their partner. Then a vicious circle leads to resentment and profound disturbance of the sexual relationship.

Actually, men and women are more alike than materialistic physiologists are ready to believe. Two individuals united in wholehearted mutual acceptance have the remarkable ability to assimilate. Then, whatever occurs in one is shared by the other. It remains one of the human miracles how human beings are capable of transmitting feelings and even thoughts to each other through the barrier of their own confining bodies. As long as they do not interfere, with their fears and apprehensions, as long as they remain receptive in full relaxation, every emotional impulse of either one affects both alike. Under such conditions, any excitement and gratification occurs simultaneously, regardless of the act or its tempo. The extent of mutual adjustment is practically unlimited. It all depends on unqualified willingness to accept each other, without demand and resentment, without complaint and discomfort. Everything is right so long as both like it. If one-sided, sexual satisfaction is always a misuse of the partner, not much different from rape.[3] Love is a mutual task; sex a mutual understanding.[4]

LOVE NEEDS CONSTANT TENDING

Husband and wife, aware of this, will try to stimulate affection, to earn responsiveness, instead of considering his or her own rights. Too many forget as soon as they are married their capacity to charm and to entice. They believe that the marriage document gives them a right to gratification. And when their expectations do not materialize, they demand more instead of seeking to attract more. Many women take great pains to make themselves attractive when they go out or visit friends, but neglect any care in the intimacy of their home life. They take their husband's love for granted instead of constantly winning his admiration and affection anew. Once married, they don't seem to care whether they excite the mate's feeling and emotions, and they forget all the many subtle means which they used so successfully to catch him. They may even consider such efforts as humiliating. No, they should be loved as they are! No woman is so young and pretty that she does not

[3] "Whosoever humiliates and deprecates his partner of the opposite sex will be denied the happiness of love." W. Beran Wolfe, *How to Be Happy though Human.* Farrar and Rinehart, New York, 1931.
[4] "Everything that grows out of the proper understanding is right, just as everything will be useless if one is not in harmony with his partner." Sofie Lazarsfeld, *Rhythm of Life,* Greenberg publisher, 1934.

need, and none so old or ugly that she cannot find, skillful methods to keep her husband's emotion alive.

Many men, on their part, behave in much the same way. After their marriage, or at least after the honeymoon is over, they forget so often the "sweet little nothings" which gave so much delight—or at least they reserve them for social occasions to demonstrate their devotion in the presence of others. They fail to realize that a woman demands signs of love and affection and cannot take anything as self-evident if it is not expressed again and again. It is neither more difficult nor less gratifying to woo a woman after the wedding. Often, however, men are not trained to do this. They consider their wives as being obliged to marital "duty" and demand sexual gratification as part of the bargain. Many of them actually think that only the masculine desire is important and that women have to accept it whenever it occurs. They believe that women should always be ready but never demand.

The conviction of their masculine superiority supports this fallacious and often fatal assumption of many men. They have not learned that responsiveness to sex is the duty of both mates, and any discord in a sex relationship must be regarded as a common problem which can be solved only if both parties unite their efforts for the common task.

EVERY PROBLEM IS A COMMON TASK

It is vital to marital happiness to recognize that any disturbing problem is a common task which calls for mutual encouragement and assistance. The most severe predicament which may befall a married couple does not neces-

164

sarily endanger the union; on the contrary, it frequently knits them more closely together. The severity of the predicament is of no significance. Everything depends solely on the ability of the mates to stick together when confronted with a difficult task. Identical points of view and a strong set of values, accepted by both, increase the resistance of a couple to any reverse. Strong religious feelings, dependable philosophic conceptions of life, shared by husband and wife, give marriage stability. That does not mean that difference in religion or conflicting convictions are necessarily a handicap. Such differences demand only a broader understanding—a well-developed sense of tolerance. That in itself implies strong moral values, which can more than make up for an otherwise detrimental incongruity.

IN-LAWS ARE A MUTUAL TASK

One of the dangerous and yet most nearly universal threats to marital harmony is provided by in-laws. Not that any predicament arising from this source is more difficult to handle than any other; but in this case the temptation is strong to blame the mate and his family for resulting frictions. The husband's mother and family is generally the more disturbing. Whereas the mother of a daughter very often welcomes a new man in the family, the mother of a son frequently considers no girl good enough for her "gem." There are, of course, many exceptions to this rule, but experience shows a slight advantage in the favor of the wife's mother. Regardless of the quarter from which the danger threatens, it will lead to friction and disappointment unless both sides deliberately decide to regard the problem as a common task. Otherwise, one blames the other for being partial and having no understanding.

Once this antagonism is established, a satisfactory solution is blocked. Trying to convince each other that he or she is wrong does not help and certainly does not make for better understanding. The wife of a mother's boy forgets too easily that he, too, suffers from her domination or indulgence, even though he himself, as a good son, may feel obliged to defend his mother against any accusation. Realizing this conflict between an admired mother and a beloved wife, a clever woman will help him, not upset him with her complaints, regardless of how justified they might be. It is not difficult to find an effective answer to a situation which many consider almost insoluble, if we only use our imagination and our intelligence in the right direction. The unquestionable differences of interest among the various members of the family may be ineradicable, at least for the present moment. But the harmony of the marriage need not necessarily suffer.

Mrs. R. came for advice: She had been married a short time, and the couple was getting along nicely. Only one problem seemed insoluble—her husband's family. She was at her wit's end and had come to find out what she could do before she made many more mistakes, which certainly would endanger her marriage. The husband had lived previously to their marriage with his sister, who had always succeeded in preventing his forming too close a relationship with any girl. Thus he was no longer young when he finally fell in love with Mrs. R., who managed through a trying courtship to win the final victory over his family ties. The sister, who feared losing his financial support, was furious. She even refused to come to the wedding.

Shortly afterward the sister reproachfully invited the husband to come to visit her. He hesitated a moment, because he resented her obstinacy—but he went. Mrs. R., who was not included in the invitation, was not too happy, as she resented the open rejection by her sister-in-law and felt that under these circumstances her husband should not go. Her resentment flared into open anger when Mr. R. returned from the visit obviously a different man. He was cold, unfriendly, irritable, and for the first time in their short marriage, the atmosphere became unpleasant and tense. The situation lasted several days. No word was spoken, and the previous harmony was restored by itself.

But the peace was only short lived and superficial. A few weeks later the sister-in-law called and invited Mr. R. again. This time Mrs. R. took a definite stand against his visits. It resulted in the first open controversy and hostility. Although he could not actually blame his wife, Mr. R. accused her of a lack of understanding because she interfered with his obligation to his family. In this situation, Mrs. R. came for help. Should she let him go and risk his being incited against her by her sister-in-law? Restoring his close relationship with his family, he might withdraw from his wife. Or should she protest against his desire to visit his sister, at the risk of open quarrels? That would not prevent her husband from secretly doing what he wanted.

I tried to make Mrs. R. understand that neither fighting nor giving in would help her. But there was another possibility. Mr. R. himself undoubtedly was in a grave conflict and did not know what to do. His devotion to his wife conflicted with his loyalty to his family. Why didn't she help him? And so Mrs. R. discovered a solution. She went home and told her husband she didn't want to alienate him from his family; but wouldn't he think it only fair to take her with him if he went visiting them? His reaction was immediate and very strong. He was deeply grateful for her willingness to go with him, after all the humiliations which she had experienced from his sister. He called his sister up immediately and asked her whether he could come with his wife. The sister found some excuse for this occasion and promised to invite him at a later date—but he never received an invitation. From this moment on all problems concerning his family were solved by husband and wife together. There never arose any difference between them from this source.

Not all conflicts about in-laws can be solved so easily. It takes more endurance and patience to meet continuously persons who regard the wife's very existence as an insult. But as long as she does not let anyone drive her from the side of her husband, as long as she tries to think in his terms, encouraging him, supporting him and helping him to overcome the conflict within himself, nothing can actually destroy their concord. Sometimes she may even be able, finally, to win over the mother-in-law, who may come to realize that she will always have to contend with her daughter-in-law and cannot extricate her from her son's heart.

This favorite solution may seem impossible at the beginning, but it can be accomplished by a brave and kind person who has sympathetic understanding even for the sufferings of those who want to humiliate and hurt her. If this is impossible, the wife may be able to convince her husband that there is no way of helping his mother, regardless of how sincerely they try to find one. Recognizing his wife as a true and sincere comrade, gaining confidence in her and strength through her, he may become able to take the natural step of establishing his own independence of his mother, an independence which more fortunate men gained under less dramatic and painful circumstances. In any case, the proper behavior of the wife, who neither gives in nor fights, but understands and helps, can restore an equilibrium between mother and son which no longer endangers the marriage.

The same is true, of course, for the wife's relatives, as far as the husband is concerned. His jealousy or possessiveness can never be justified because he feels rejected or even humiliated by his in-laws. If he believes he can demand submission of his wife, if he considers it a feminine duty for a girl to leave her family and follow her husband, he shows no understanding of her human constitution. He may enforce submission, but he will reap the hostility which he has sown. Demands as a means of solving difficulties are not less futile if the man thinks he has a right to make them. Unfortunately, men are often not ready to give courage and comfort to their wives in their predicaments and conflicts. It looks as if a certain concept of masculine superiority deters men from showing sympathy and understanding. Sensitivity for their prestige is too easily aroused, and they seem to owe it to their dignity to demand and to enforce submission. Thus, although the problem may appear due to the in-laws, in reality it has been created by the domineering and demanding behavior of the husband.

ECONOMIC DIFFICULTIES

The same care is needed to distinguish the real problem from the apparent one in analyzing any other source of marital discord. Economic difficulties are frequently blamed for destroying harmony. "When poverty comes in the door, love flies out the window." It sounds good—but is it true? I have seen many marriages in which economic strain prevented disruption—and not only because the couple could no longer afford the cost of divorce. And it is probably not merely the increased ability to meet expenses which raises the number of divorces during prosperity.

Hardship can bring two people closer together as well as break their marital ties. The depression deepened some unions, and broke others. Any kind of misfortune is a test of the courage and sincerity of the mates; it is a test of the fundaments on which the marriage is built. If the wife has married only for the purpose of financial security, then of course the loss of an adequate income removes the only basis on which this particular marriage rests. On the other hand, if there is a feeling of belonging, hardship will strengthen it. Under really trying conditions many minor frictions, which often are more detrimental to the mutual understanding, disappear. Real disaster leaves no room for concern with personal prestige. Any desire of being better, any fear of appearing inferior, loses all meaning when very existence is threatened physically, economically, or socially. Women previously concerned with amusement, appearance, and luxury become real companions of their husbands, sacrificing comfort in assisting them, and even providing financial support. Many a couple under such circumstances have detected favorable qualities and traits in each other which they had never suspected before.

It cannot be denied, however, that economic troubles are only too often the immediate grounds for the collapse of the marriage. But experience has taught us to look beyond immediate conflicts for deeper reasons. As we have said before, perhaps the foundations of such a union were never broad enough to withstand any strain, or they were already so deteriorated by other frictions that the slightest additional burden completed the destruction. We must always suspect behind any marital collapse the arch-enemy of human cooperation: over-emphasis of personal prestige. How can economic hardship affect personal prestige? To understand this question we must recognize the deeper source of many marital discords which seem to be based on economic difficulties.

THE MAN AS PROVIDER

Prevalent conceptions of rights and duties for men and women give financial matters a peculiar tinge. Many a woman considers her social value in terms of the dollars which a man spends on her, be he husband or boy friend. The reduced financial capacity of the husband appears as an intolerable injury to social prestige. Any man who dares endanger her vanity and threaten her social status has to bear the full brunt of her contempt and indignation. On this basis personal quarrels and mutual accusations start. But there is another side to the picture. Men very often consider their own position correlated to the money they make. This conception is so common, at least it was so before the depression, that any man who doesn't earn or have money is regarded as a failure. Being without a job is still more difficult for a man to bear than for a woman. The deep feeling of personal inadequacy on the side of a husband who has lost his job or fortune increases the intensity of his fight for personal prestige within the family and disturbs deeply the marital equilibrium.

If the husband does not or cannot support the family adequately, it takes much courage and a deep sense of dignity on both sides to maintain the marital harmony. The wife is inclined to regard his shortcoming as a personal insult, often interpreting the man's failure to make more money as a neglect of wife and family. The husband, on his side, feels his inadequacy deeply, even if his pride prevents him from revealing his feeling of shame. But his actions

171

demonstrate clearly his futile and disturbing attempts to compensate for his alleged failure. He may remonstrate actively or passively by staying in bed and refusing any kind of contribution on his side; or he may play the tyrant, demanding and ordering the other members of the family around. The wife generally doesn't understand at all why he behaves as he does; and her anger increases when he becomes less and less willing to help at home. She thinks that he should feel *more* obliged to assume domestic duties if he isn't working. She does not realize that his conception of domestic work as being feminine and therefore inferior deepens his feeling of shame. Her nagging drives him deeper into desperate opposition.

If men were trained to consider housework as not inferior, and women regarded support of the family as not exclusively a man's job, then unemployment of the husband would hardly create any problem. The situation is somewhat different among professional men, where the husband's importance as artist, actor, writer, lawyer, or scientist is less dependent upon the amount of money he makes. In this and similar fields a man may gain professional status and still be poor, and the wife can be proud of him, even though she supports him. Women and men in this group often look down upon men whose only contribution is support.

Changes in the conception of man as the only provider lead to new difficulties in another direction. Many a man resents the desire of his wife to work outside the home and to earn money herself. He regards it as a personal humiliation if his wife works. Actually it is a struggle for supremacy and prestige which prevents many a man from consenting

172

to his wife's career. To overcome such an obstacle is not easy for a woman who has something to contribute and looks for personal recognition. Neither fighting nor giving in will help. Fighting may lead to a disruption of the marital ties. Even if she wins he will continuously resent her success and, in some cases, may become so discouraged in the competition with his wife that his own efficiency is impaired. And her surrender may entail the cultivation of a resentment that will lead her either to an unhappy, empty life, or to other expressions of independence as distasteful to her jealous husband.

The clash between spouses does not preclude an agreement resulting in some satisfactory equilibrium. Many women capable and desirous of a career renounce it voluntarily because they realize how disturbing it would be for their husbands' development. Such a decision, however, cannot be regarded as "surrender." It is made deliberately in full consciousness of the benefits obtained. But if the woman is sincerely interested in some work and determined to carry it on, her giving in to threats or intimidation will not solve the problem. She should find means of maintaining her marriage along with developing a career. This requires the ability to win her husband's approval. Arguments and tears, threats and accusations, will only antagonize. Courageous women engaged in a career can be kind and firm enough to convince a husband that he does not lose anything, not even his masculine superiority, if she finds her own field of activity.

Regardless of whether the conflict is created by the husband's failure to provide or by his desire to be the only provider, the same principles are valid and should be observed if disaster is to be avoided. First of all, the wife must recognize her husband's problem and help him to solve it. He needs encouragement even if—no, *because*—he tries to play the tyrant. The husband who prevents his wife from having a career demonstrates thereby his discouragement, his fear that he will be unable to maintain his superiority. Proving to him how wrong he is in his demands proves only how right he is in questioning her devotion. Whenever problems of prestige, of distrust, or of lack of faith arise, logical arguments are of no avail. Humiliation cannot be avoided by humiliating the other one. Expressions of sincere affection, demonstrations of love, strengthen the feeling of belonging and prepare for mutual agreement. In an atmosphere of frank confidence, the most controversial issues can be settled. Of course, a wife who does not believe that her husband will ever agree, or that she will ever be able to make him understand her point of view, prepares only for a fight and disappointment.

THE STRATEGIC POSITION OF THE WIFE

Doubt in the partner, very often based on an unconscious desire to prove one's own superiority, is frequently the moving force behind apparently inevitable predicaments. The wife of a drunkard, object of public sympathy and admiration for her endurance and faithfulness, frequently has contributed more to the family situation than anyone suspects. Often enough, an ambitious and efficient woman chooses a weak and unstable husband. While she prides herself on her intention to guide and "save" him, she actually acclaims only her own virtuousness over his wickedness. This kind of woman makes it difficult for any man to be good. He has

174

no chance of competing with her impressive virtue, and punishing her with his expected misbehavior is only a small consolation. He rarely realizes that by torturing her he only adds to her glory. The wife of a drunkard is often a typical martyr; the more she suffers, the holier she becomes.

In the history of such a marriage, we find many periods in which a wife could have stopped the husband from drinking. A certain firmness could have made him aware of the consequences of his behavior—losing her, at a time when he still cared for her and yet had not been sufficiently antagonized by her contempt and nagging. But after each quarrel, after every threat, she gave in, believing his promises which she knew would never be kept. Treating drunkards requires influencing their wives first. The woman's holiness and the man's viciousness fit together and are typical of martyrdom. The peculiar equilibrium is never the fault of the man alone.

Although it may sound as if one could put the blame for these conflicts on women, we know that right and wrong are never exclusively one sided. But unfortunately, women suffer most from marital discord. Their personal dependency upon marital concord makes them more sensitive to harmony—and gives them also more responsibility. As a matter of fact, the fate of a marriage generally depends much more upon the behavior of the wife than upon that of the man. Women have, for centuries, been trained in domesticity. Their "natural" interest in marital affairs can be overcome only by a very strong masculine protest. Women have been and still are the dominated sex; but they always were the power behind the throne. This position has induced women to use other methods than the crude, forthright aggressiveness permitted to men. The scheming qualities, which have inspired their comparison with cats, compensate for their lack of actual power. Men dance as women play the tune, rather than vice versa. This does not mean that women do not need as much encouragement and assistance as men, but women reveal their need for protection readily, whereas men are prevented from doing so by their masculine pride. Often the strongest man is fundamentally like a child, and the weakest woman can have the persuasive influence of a mother. That is the reason why we must assist women in managing their husbands, rather than wait until men learn to regard their wives as partners.

This ability to lead the partner toward a common goal is necessary whenever conflicting interests appear. There are always conflicting interests, as we cannot expect two persons to have the same desires, interests, concerns, and to enjoy the same amusements and diversions. In some cases, the field of common interests is broad, in others narrow. There is no question that it is easier to maintain mutual participation when the marriage starts out with a broad basis in mutually shared goals; but in every case each mate has to enlarge his own field of interest to accord with the previous training, activity, and concern of the partner. It seems less advisable to demand that anyone should cut out previous interests because they are distasteful to the other one. The positive desire should have more weight than the negative distaste, because overcoming an original distaste broadens the base of agreement, whereas abandoning a desire narrows that base and makes for resentment. Such an adaptation, educationally considered, provides growth, and, psychologically considered, a sense of accomplishment, as well as enhancement of social worth. Each mate should be ready to give activities liked by the other a fair trial. Sincere effort to participate will make it easier to abandon some activities if they prove to be too difficult or too foreign to the mate.

Our present marital situation demands, for more than one reason, that woman take the lead, not only because by her training and inheritance she is generally more apt to induce and influence, but also because at the present time women generally have more inclination than men to broaden their interests. If the husband is an artist, scientist, or works in a special cultural field, then he generally stimulates the interest of his wife in his activities. If he cannot do so, his marriage is bound to fail. But too many American men are interested only in business and work. Outside interests are limited to politics and recreation with men friends in drinking and playing. Interest in art, books, music, psychology, and other cultural activities is increasingly—and unfortunately—becoming the privilege of women. Few men complain that their wives want to stay home, refuse to go to a concert or art exhibit, but women very frequently voice such grievances.

STIMULATING NEW INTERESTS

Whoever desires the participation, initially rejected by the partner, must first win him over. Demands create opposition, mutual resentment and disappointment. One woman complained that her husband was interested only in reading the papers and showed no appreciation of good books. The other day, she reported, she read to him an introduction to philosophy, a rather heavy book. She noticed that he didn't listen, and she repeated the page. After he gave more definite signs of his displeasure she gave up—angrily, of course—any further attempt to introduce him to good books. Certain futile attempts to introduce a husband to arts or books let one suspect that the wife is neither completely blameless nor as sincerely worried about his lack of interest as she believed. On the contrary, a certain deep satisfaction very often is the undertone of the complaint, revealing her satisfaction with her superiority. Moreover, her attempts were the more discouraging and threatening to her husband's self-esteem because they occurred precisely at the point where he needed careful help to overcome previously produced discouragement and faulty training.

It is not a question of technique—of *how;* it is the attitude that determines success or failure. Real love and devotion, sincere appreciation and respect, lead to mutual gratification and compliance. Genuine interest in one's partner will help in recognizing even without academic training in psychology why the husband is reluctant to entertain friends or attend parties. His being tired is not the real cause: if he enjoyed social contact more, he would not feel tired. A card game with friends, for instance, might awaken his energy immediately. But outside of that he feels "bored." He may have nothing in common with certain guests because he has not been trained for social participation. He may consider that just being with others is a waste of time, because nothing tangible results from such an activity. He may be a materialist and may regard material accomplishments as the only things valuable in life. Or perhaps he wants to excel, and though perfectly well trained to play the first role in his job, in his family, and among those associates who appreciate him, he feels lost among a larger group of social acquaintances. No one pays any special attention to him, and he may not be able to compete with the social skill and resourcefulness of others.

A wife who has natural sympathy and understanding for her husband will manage to arrange social contacts in such a manner that they will give him some satisfaction. She will carefully try to change his outlook, perhaps, and may be able to introduce previously unknown and unrecognized values into his life. Why should it be easier to make a husband discover the pleasure of a good home, of well-cooked meals, than the pleasure of a good book, when he has not experienced either one before? Some might say that while he may not have experienced a good home-cooked meal previously, he certainly has eaten before. Such objections cannot stand, for the parallel goes further; as he has eaten before, but not good food, so he certainly also has read, but not good material. He may also have heard music and perhaps even enjoyed it, but never experienced finer music. He must learn to enjoy good music, which the wife likes, the type of food she cooks, the books she admires.

In this situation, the crux may well be that the wife truly desires that her husband recognize the quality of her cooking, for such recognition enhances her prestige. If she really desires him to like "good" books, she might make her appeal on the ground of the importance of his point of view to supplement her own; or to enjoy certain company, to show her own enjoyment incomplete unless supplemented by his special way of evaluating their opinions, etc. Fundamen-

179

tally, her appeal must honestly enhance his self-esteem, not diminish it.

Anything new is at first distasteful. It is strange, bewildering. Taste in general is very much influenced by repeated experience, by training. If, in introducing some new experience in anyone's life, one is not careful to make that experience pleasant, then one must expect to spend more time and effort to overcome a reinforced natural initial dislike. A wife who wants her husband to enjoy a concert, when he never previously "understood" classical music, has to move slowly. She must be careful in selecting the program, and must also consider some other stimulation. That should not be difficult, so long as he likes her company and enjoys satisfying her. But too many women diminish their chances of success by condescension—because they regard the man's business world as inferior. They frown upon his resistance to higher cultural values; instead of appreciating the difficulties a man has to overcome, they resent his apprehension and hesitance. Thus what should be a source of mutual enjoyment becomes a bone of contention—a very unpleasant duty on one side, and a denied "right" on the other.

Although it is more generally the wife who tries to induce the husband, in some cases the man is the more culturally interested partner. In any case, he wants his wife to share his interests, which may be new to her. As a rule, women have far less difficulty in submerging in a man's interests and activity than do men in women's. When a woman likes a man, she feels no threat to her prestige in following his lead, even into interests which are considered predominantly masculine, like sports, athletics. Only if his hobbies take him away from her and do not permit sharing his enjoyment (such as stamp collecting, handicraft, carpentry, and technical "tinkering"), is she likely to resent his recreational activities.

Where neither partner interferes, where each shows tolerance and understanding, each partner may enjoy pleasures which the other one either cannot or does not want to share. The presence of "antagonistic" interests, therefore, is never the cause of disappointment, but always the consequence of impaired cooperation and a deteriorated interest in each other. Indeed, very often strong interests in the same field and even common work might offer much more opportunity for friction and tension, especially if competition develops. A couple, happily married for some years, develops identical interests just in the course of living together. Their shared experiences, the turn of events, pleasant and unpleasant impressions, gratifications and worries, are strong ties which finally, in old age, make them not only act but even look alike. Such coalescence is a result of more than habit. It is broader and goes deeper, this becoming used to liking and disliking the same things, this regarding life, in its big aspects and its small routine, from the same point of view. The development of identical interests is natural, yet it implies genuine efforts to iron out antagonisms which may interfere and to make leisure time a pleasant experience for both.

A typical example of contradictory interests and their detrimental effect upon marital harmony is the case of Mrs. D. She is a young woman with wide and liberal interests. She married the brother of her best girl friend. As she and her friend were very congenial in their interests and likes, she expected the brother to be like his sister. During a short courtship he was very attentive, sharing her activities. They married while he was in the Army, shortly before he left for overseas duty. When he came back, they really got acquainted with each other—and then her disappointment began. She found that he had little interest in classical music, only in light operettas, and that his political beliefs opposed those held by her and her family. She felt cheated and hurt; the more she argued and criticized him for his reluctance to enjoy a concert, the stronger he stuck to his guns. Their arguments and frictions affected shortly their sexual relationship. She lost interest—he demanded more; she felt abused and ceased responding. At this point, when she came for advice, she had begun to give serious consideration to obtaining a divorce.

After listening to all her complaints, I suggested an interview with both of them present. In the following three-way discussion, it became apparent that he was very much in love with her, was himself happy and could not understand why she was not. He expressed willingness to do whatever was necessary. But she maintained that he had promised cooperation before and had failed to keep his promises. He admitted that he did not know why he could not refrain from antagonizing her, why, though he wanted to comply with her wishes, he by no means always did so.

It became clear that she was completely right in her complaints; on the logical level he was wrong. But psychologically she was the cause of all their conflicts. Her resentment, her pressure and disapproval were the real causes of the friction and endangered her marriage. As she was the key person, as the whole fate of this union depended upon her attitude alone since he was willing to get along, I suggested that she was the person in need of help.

After only a few consultations the situation changed completely. As she came to recognize her own part in the dirty game, she stopped provoking and resenting. The first effect was an immediate improvement of their relationship. They became friendly and mutually affectionate again. Since she again responded sexually, he ceased demanding so much. From then on she learned to approach her husband in a different way. She realized that she could just as well sympathize with his difficulties in sitting through a heavy program when they went to a concert, instead of arguing with him and assuring him that he did not understand the beauty of the music. In political discussions she could call on him to express his points of view, appreciating the fact that she had an expert from the other side of the fence, instead of scolding him about his wrong views. She recognized that, while she accused him of undemocratic attitudes, her own attitude of intolerance toward his political outlook could certainly not be considered democratic. With such an attitude of appreciation on her part, it could be expected that his own opinions and tastes would gradually change and approximate hers, since her violent and humiliating disapproval was the main force that kept him in opposition for the sake of his pride and self-esteem.

The decisive factor in the rehabilitation of this marriage was Mrs. D.'s recognition that logical right is not enough, that she had first to accept him as he was—and that she had to start with herself, considering only what she could do.

RECREATION AND SOCIAL PARTICIPATION

Today, more than previously, we recognize the importance of recreation for a well-balanced life. Constructive use of spare time is as much a duty as finding an adequate job. Unless we organize our recreation successfully, we are neither capable of giving our best to our work, nor do we fulfill our obligations to friends and to the family. It is the duty of every married couple not only to learn how to work together, but also how to enjoy life together.

Is it possible, however, to enjoy life today, when misery surrounds us and friction and hatred are rampant? There are many ways to enjoy life—all types of joy. Joy can be loud or quiet, passionate or calm, but it always indicates a great amount of acceptance. People who are not in opposition to life, whose emotions are not based on resentment, cannot but enjoy living. They can enjoy each other in

183

erotic and sexual play, they can enjoy being together, regardless of what each is doing. They enjoy going places together, and they enjoy developing new interests where old ones permit expansion. But they should never forget that marriage cannot replace the larger community to which each human being belongs—friends, group, nation, mankind.

Regardless of how happy two persons may be with each other, if they are united in mutual defiance of the rest of the world, they pay for it. A marriage which has as its foundation retreat from others may provide deep satisfaction for both mates; but one will have to survive the other and will not find his way back to life. If they have children, they will protect them against the demand of the outer world; they are bound to suffer, whether they succeed in alienating the children from, or whether they lose them to, the world. The intimate unit of two persons must be imbedded in a larger unit, provided by friends and groups, to which both belong. Social contact with friends, social activities, uniting one couple with others, must supplement home life, as work and recreation supplement each other. Neglect of either is harmful.

Social contact and interest in religion, in art, in science, as well as in politics, are not the fanciful ambitions of either husband or wife; they represent a broad foundation for the feeling of belonging to a greater unit than marriage. The tendency of either to keep aloof from the rest of the world indicates deep hostility and lack of social interest. Through the activities mentioned, we participate practically or in spirit with others. We share their thoughts and their work. We become actually a part of mankind, and our marriage becomes integrated itself in the stream of evolution, in which all of mankind is involved. The more the marriage is engulfed in this current, the more it is a part of life as a whole, the more stable and secure is its course. Good friends, devoted to husband and wife alike, are an invaluable help in times of distress. Common friends not only enrich the marital atmosphere, but function also as a cushion against the difficulties, disappointments, conflicts, and antagonisms which cannot be completely avoided when two people live together.

THE REAL REASON FOR DISAPPOINTMENTS

Behind a concrete problem and overt friction are general attitudes and erroneous conceptions. Many disappointments derive from comparing past expectations with present circumstances. Unfortunately, both are often misinterpreted. We rarely are aware of what we expected, and we frequently misjudge what we have. Our experiences are in line with what we actually anticipated, only we fail to recognize our expectations and our own contribution to present disappointments. We confuse wishful thinking with actual expectation, and when the event deviates from our desire, we do not blame our own planning but factors outside ourselves. We all want peace and happiness, but do we actually anticipate them? Rarely—and, therefore, we do little to attain them.

We frequently act as if everything must go wrong, and as if happiness were not attainable. We don't even expect ourselves to act properly, because we don't believe in our ability to meet difficulties adequately. We do not admit how much we ourselves contribute to existing problems and difficulties. We feel provoked and do not realize how much we ourselves provoke.

As long as we maintain some kind of confidence and hope, we can bear disappointment and dissatisfaction. But there comes a moment when we have the feeling that we cannot bear it any longer, that something is broken within ourselves—that some irreparable damage is done. Nothing actually is irreparable. But this, sometimes even physical, feeling of an inner collapse indicates determination to withdraw, refusal to continue to cooperate. The actual occasion is never the cause, it is only the last burden, too much strain for an already frayed bond. An individual who does not lose courage, to whom problems exist only to be solved, never experiences this feeling of giving up. Never will he permit himself to drift farther and farther away from his companion.

Our own actions and attitudes influence not only the conditions in which we live, but also the behavior of the persons around us. In a good marriage both partners become better human beings merely by living together. In an unsuccessful marriage, each evokes the worst qualities in the other. As a consequence, character and the impulse to cooperate deteriorate. The destructive influence of enmity, repression, and accusation leads to mutual evasion of responsibility. Both partners feel insecure and are stimulated to acts of annoyance, punishment, and revenge. Each becomes what the other expects him to be, and that, unfortunately, is generally not good. However, both agree on one point, namely, that the other one is wrong.

FINDING SOLUTIONS

We must be emphatic: These statements are not theoretical but have very practical implications. We can change our whole life and the attitude of people around us simply by changing ourselves. The change is not easy. Improvement is possible only when the necessity to start with oneself is recognized—and admitted. Too many persons try to educate and change the partner. How many even enter marriage with the idea of changing the other one! In living together we do influence and change each other— but not by insisting upon a change of the partner. Only by our own behavior can we influence those with whom we live.

Whatever happens in a marital relationship expresses the interaction of both spouses. Instead of the general demand, "If only he would change, I'd be glad to act differently," we should recognize the truth that "If I change my behavior, he cannot continue his." Even the slightest changes in attitude of one are immediately reflected in the behavior of the other. Without realizing it, we possess uncanny sensibility and remarkable powers of coordination. Unfortunately, we know much better how to fight and how to hurt than how to please. Therefore, we are more efficient and successful in warfare and fighting. It generally takes more time and effort to provoke pleasant reactions, especially when warfare has already begun. In the marriage relationship, a certain amount of fight, of competition, of hostility and distrust, exists often from the beginning; and it takes deliberate effort to establish an atmosphere of genuine trust and kindness.

187

Not that most people are bad or malicious. All possibilities for good or bad exist in almost every human being. Husband and wife have the power of arousing the good or bad in each other. But what do they know of each other? They live together in one room, they eat at the same table, they share the same bed, their whole life is intimately fused by mutual activity—yet how little they understand one another! Each knows the other's habits (mostly annoying), peculiarities, preferences, and irritabilities. What has all this to do with the deeper personality, with expectations and fears, with conceptions of life and of one's self, with all that which makes people act and behave in a definite way? Husband and wife recognize symptoms, but not the forces behind them. And if they are disappointed, they wish to eliminate the symptoms without being willing to gratify the needs in each other.

Curiously enough, too often after two individuals have separated, they understand each other better than before. Friction, mutual fear, the fight for prestige, had blinded them. In blaming each other, they sought to excuse their own maladjustments. Ignoring or riding roughshod over the partner's fundamental needs made it easier to continue fighting for one's own ends. What each says about the other is generally right, although statements seem to contradict each other. But it is not important who is right and who is wrong. Each is right from his own point of view, and wrong from the other's. The point is that if we love someone, we do not ask if he is right or wrong. That is why love is called blind. But love is not necessarily blind. Love says, "I love you, although you are not perfect. I love you and accept you as you are." But later, when our self-esteem and prestige are threatened, we do not take each other as we are. In fighting for our own superiority we find faults in our partner and use them as good reasons for stopping our own cooperation. For happiness, the question of rightness and wrongness is unimportant. But to accept the other's faults and virtues—that is important.

We must start at this point when discord and disappointment threaten the very existence of a marriage—or, in minor degrees, just make it less comfortable and satisfactory. The first step, the first condition for any improvement, means accepting the situation, however unpleasant, as it is; it is futile to wish it were different. To face the problem squarely and courageously is the prerequisite for finding the ways and means out of a predicament. It is not always easy, as we are timid. But running away never pays; no problem is solved in that way. When we have decided to face the issue, when we muster our courage and try to think in terms of "What can *I* do to improve the situation?"—then we are on the right track. Having abandoned the illusion that we may succeed by fighting and forcing the issue, having overcome our feeling of inadequacy, having admitted that the other one suffers too, we discover solutions. Perhaps slowly, perhaps inadequately at first, but with growing courage as our insight increases and our growing self-confidence makes us less vulnerable and more effective.

The following example is characteristic of thousands of episodes and conflicts found in the history of almost every marriage. They could have been avoided or easily solved had both spouses understood the underlying motives and goals of each other, had they refrained from resenting and

189

accusing each other and looked instead for their own chances to change the situation.

Mrs. M. came for advice in a matter that seemed to her thoroughly trivial and yet was threatening her whole marriage. Married about one year, she got along very well with her husband. Sexually and socially they had fun together and were devoted companions—except for one disagreement which lately had taken on such proportions that the harmony between them was gone, affecting almost every phase of their marital life. She reported that despite all her efforts she was unable to make Mr. M. give her her weekly allowance for food and other housekeeping expenses on time. She had to ask for the money each week, several times; and, if she did not ask, he "forgot" altogether to give her her money until the week was over. She talked to him, pleaded with him, threatened him—nothing helped. The more they quarreled, the less he obliged. What could she do? Now he had started to accuse her of spending too much; she should have saved something from last week. "From my fifteen dollars a week!—when I try so hard to make ends meet since he simply refuses to give me more." She could not understand why he was so miserly in this regard, since he spent rather generously on her otherwise.

What could she do to avoid the fighting, quarreling and invariable final submission to the humiliating experience? We can well understand her predicament. It was impossible for her to plan her budget and even her meals. She had to borrow and to make debts, both of which she hated. What could she have done instead of talking, pleading—and threatening?

Here we reach the crucial point. Despite the fact that the majority of housewives probably would have acted as Mrs. M. did, they all miss the boat. A little understanding of the little guy who wants to play the big boss would have saved many sleepless nights, tortuous scenes, wasted hours, days, and weeks. It is obvious that the "unreasonable" behavior of Mr. M. appears only unreasonable when looked upon at the logical level. He certainly had not the "right" nor any logical reason to behave as he did. But the situation looks different when regarded from the psychological point of view. He loved his

190

wife dearly, was devoted to her to such a degree that she could wind him around her little finger. And she did so, except in this one field of action. The only point where he could exert his superiority was in his role as provider. And—without being aware of it—he wanted to make full use of this one advantage. He wanted to be asked, to be begged. If he had given her her allowance at the beginning of the week, without any ado, then even this sign of his authority would have been taken away from him. Instead of power he would have accepted just another duty. He could not explain that to her, because he was not aware of his psychological motivation. Therefore, when she accused him, he had to come back with rationalizations, with flimsy retaliations and unfounded reproaches, which made Mrs. M. only more furious. And so they became deadlocked in a battle which could result only in the break-up of their marriage.

Once Mrs. M. realized the situation, overcame her hurt pride and resentment, she found easily what *she* could do to solve the problem. First, she no longer resented asking him for what she knew was due her. She wanted him to be happy —and if that was what made him happy, why not give it to him. It was so easy, once her false pride was gone. Still, there remained some difficulty. She had to ask him several times for the money, of course, as he did not give it to her immediately. That sometimes involved hardships as bills had to be paid. What to do? But Mrs. M., clever as she was, found a simple answer. She discovered that she could as easily get from him a hundred dollars as fifteen dollars if she asked for it several times. He actually was very generous. So on several occasions she got a hundred dollars, which gave her a reserve to fall back on if he did not provide the weekly allowance on time. And reproaches and scenes were never necessary.

What she had learned from this experience went deeper than the successful handling of the allowance problem. She discovered that their real danger lay in their mutual competition, that he was afraid of being just a "sucker," that his love and devotion would make him her slave, and that she wanted, more than necessary, her queenly position, ambitious and pampered as she was. In the limelight of the one conflict, she learned to understand the deeper conflict endangering their

191

entire relationship—and she found the way of solving the *whole* problem.

MARITAL CONSULTATION SERVICE

Since it is difficult to understand one's self and one's mate, the necessity arises to consult someone whose training enables him to assist in the process of mutual adjustment. The psychiatrist renders service to "normal" persons in their normal problems. Psychiatry is no longer a science concerned mainly with diagnosing and curing insanity and abnormalities. From the analysis of slightly maladjusted persons has come a new knowledge of human nature. We have today available techniques to understand human personalities and human behavior, an understanding important for the daily problems of the normal (that means average) individual. Wherever a deeper understanding of human problems is necessary, the psychiatric approach will be useful and sometimes essential. Husbands or wives in their sincere desire to overcome dangerous predicaments, in their endeavor to correct and overcome existing difficulties, look for the help which psychiatry can give, in what can be called marital consultations. Psychiatric training enables non-medical persons also to render such services. Ministers and lawyers, social workers and educators—all those who in the exercise of their professions meet human beings in distress, need training in understanding personalities.

In all cases, however, where emotional upset, disappointment, and failure lead to deeper disturbance of the whole personality and to the establishment of various emotional and nervous symptoms, consultation of a psychiatrist is required. This comparatively new idea of establishing clinics for marital consultation, where psychiatrist and social worker, psychologist and sociologist work together to assist individuals and couples,[5] to give general information and to offer adequate advice, is in line with the development of mental and social hygiene, of public welfare and family service. Such a project may find some opposition from various fields, but it is the result of an increasing awareness of the general and social nature of marital problems and of a tendency to organize vital assistance for the great public. It may be expected that this new venture will increasingly become part of our social institutions.

DIVORCE AS A MARITAL PROBLEM

Yet all available advice and all knowledge and instruction will not prevent the occurrence of marital situations so tense and full of antagonism that it seems impossible to maintain a satisfactory marriage. Whether we believe in divorce or not, there undeniably are marriages which threaten not only the welfare but the mental and sometimes even physical well-being of adults and children; separation seems then to be the only solution for survival. On the other hand, we cannot doubt that divorces are often sought where an adjustment could be made, either with some sincere intention or by seeking adequate assistance. There is no general rule of when and under what circumstances divorce is justified. It seems, however, that usually the more courageous solution is also the better one. Some contem-

[5] Dr. Paul Popenoe was a pioneer in this field when he organized in 1930 the Institute of Family Relations in Los Angeles for personal services, public education, and research.

193

plate divorce because they are cowards and wish to evade the task of submitting, contributing, and accepting. Others avoid divorce and continue a miserable, devastating marriage because they are afraid of facing life alone, of taking on responsibility to care for themselves and their children. Whatever is accomplished on the basis of fear is dangerous and increases suffering and misery.

It depends on each situation which solution requires courage and self-confidence. That is one aspect which may lead to recognition of adequate procedure. But it is still only one aspect—it cannot alone decide the issue. The interest of all the persons involved must be considered; first of all, the interests of children, where there are any. A home full of friction and humiliation, abuse and brutality is worse than a rather peaceful home atmosphere with only one parent. It cannot be doubted that both parents have definite contributions to make in the rearing of children, but harmony and the spirit of love and kindness are more important than anything else. Any person with a feeling of responsibility will deliberate thoroughly before breaking up a marriage. It seems always advisable to seek expert opinion before making any decisive step, as it is always difficult to evaluate properly any situation where personal interests and emotions are involved.

It must not be overlooked that divorce itself is a marital problem and hence can be solved only by cooperation between husband and wife. In any marriage, it is the last cooperative effort; but for many, it is also the first. If husband and wife cannot be brought to the realization that divorce is a common task which must be solved cooperatively by both, the divorce procedure may easily become a source of continued friction, hardship, and misery. In these cases, the marital conflict may continue long after the marriage itself has ceased to exist, especially if there are children.

Although the decision as to whether or not divorce is justified lies officially with the judge, he is hardly in a position to know all the factors. It should not be up to the law alone to forbid or permit divorces. Any regulation which does not take into consideration the social and psychological factors leading to friction and disappointment must do injustice in certain cases. Without direct insight into the situation, without sufficient opportunity to analyze the deeper psychological problems and the persons involved, no one can decide upon the advisability of a divorce. There seems to be a solution for avoiding the deplorable consequences of either granting or refusing a divorce on legal grounds alone, namely instituting obligatory marital consultation which offers opportunity for individual examination. Each person involved must have the right to decide for himself whether he or she is willing to maintain marital obligations; the good will of the partners linked in matrimony is indispensable for any kind of cooperation.

In former times, when people were more accustomed than now to submit themselves to strong personal regulations, it was possible by forbidding divorce to make men and women more ready to accept any existing marital conditions. As they had no chance to separate, they probably were more inclined to make the best of any situation which fate or their own good or bad efforts had established. In our times individuals are conceded the right to express themselves freely. Hence any attempt from the outside to force the decision must increase tension and opposition.

Today there is no chance of preventing divorces by forbidding them by law. The resulting feeling of resentment would intensify the antagonism against the mate, against the prevailing marital situation, and against the whole institution of marriage. Actions based on such emotions would hardly please those likely to favor a strict law against divorce.

We cannot conclude this chapter without discussing some of the problems that arise after the divorce. Once "freedom" has been obtained, does the divorcé return to the state of a person single and unmarried? No. More than likely his sense of self-esteem has been badly shaken. In our competitive mode of living our sense of personal worth depends upon what we call our "success." Whatever is regarded as failure reflects on our whole value. Prestige seems to be more important than any other quality or capacity. Divorce is frequently regarded as a personal failure. Especially women are receptive to such an erroneous evaluation. They regard a feeling of insecurity as a logical consequence of being divorced. Such a feeling, however, reflects only a doubt in one's self, an exaggerated desire for protection, and an apprehension of public disapproval and disdain. As a consequence, divorce appears as a humiliation. Little confident in their own future, and convinced of their apparently hopeless plight, many divorced women either withdraw completely from attempting a new and better founded marriage, or seek superficial and cheap compensations.

A proper evaluation of their previous marital experiences might easily smoothe the way in a new marriage. The past can equally well serve as a source of fear or as the basis for a better understanding and a more mature outlook. It all depends on the conclusion we draw from previous mistakes. Our attitude toward love and sex reflects our general outlook on life; our relationship to persons of the opposite sex expresses our general attitude toward all other human beings. A woman who participates in human endeavor and who takes an active part in progress and evolution will always find her place in the world, even if she is divorced. Men rarely regard divorce as evidence of failure and misfortune, and are more apt to make full use of their new freedom. They, not the wife or the children, are generally the first to see the "green light," to emerge from friction and previous disappointments, and to take full advantage of new possibilities.

WOMAN'S PLACE IS IN THE COMMUNITY

Divorce is only one situation in which a wrong social attitude of women manifests itself. In previous times, when the attitude toward woman strictly relegated her to the family circle, allowing her no function and no status outside of her family, she could and should have only one interest: husband and children. In her case, divorce ended her career. Today such an attitude, although frequently observed, is not only unjustified, but actually detrimental. Women, brought up and kept in such dependency on husband and family in a society which no longer is strictly patriarchal, are endangered in their future mental and emotional health and their human functioning. They are not only unprepared for the possibility of divorce which today becomes more frequent; their fear of such a possible failure makes them tense and apprehensive and often enough diminishes their ability to prevent the anticipated catastrophe in marriage. Their inability to recognize their function outside of the family leads to another more frequent and more disastrous consequence.

The number of women who break down around the period of climacteric is increasing alarmingly. Many physicians are inclined to attribute the mental and emotional breakdown at that time to the changes in the endocrine system, as if the "change of life" meant only a biological change in the functions of the glands. Careful studies and observations of patients suffering from involutional melancholia, which may vary in degree from slight depressions to fully developed psychoses, reveal that the disturbing factor is not so much the upset biological equilibrium within the body as the change in the life situations to which these patients are exposed. These disturbances are mostly found in women who have been excellent wives and mothers and who suddenly find themselves without any function in life. Their breakdown generally occurs when the children have grown up and left home. Their role as grandmothers does not satisfy them since modern parents do not permit grandparents to meddle in their affairs and keep their children away from this pampering influence. The husband, who found his own place in his business and in his social activities, cannot again pay the same attention and affection to his wife as he did when they were first married. The wife has devoted most of her time and interest to the care of the children; now she has a great deal of time on her hands and does not know what to do with it. She still has work to do in her home, of course. But this job is no longer significant and meaningful. To take care of herself and of her husband, with all the facilities of housekeeping available, does not require all her qualities and energies. So she thinks about a job. But, even if she has spent some hours on volunteer work, she has no training, no skill for any important position. She can only accept a minor position without power and responsibility, which contrasts sharply with her domestic role as queen, which she has occupied for many years.

In this predicament, without hope for any future, these women break down; and, ironically, they are often the best and most capable ones. The domestic role, still required of many women, even of those with college education, wastes their capacities for functioning within society at large. A re-education of parents, of husbands and wives is necessary to prepare our generation of girls and women for the necessary functioning outside their families. Many of the best qualities of women are ignored or wasted when they are not prepared to tackle a significant job outside of home. While society loses their valuable contributions, they themselves are unprepared for any event whereby they lose their position in life, be it divorce, maturity of children, or death of the husband. This last is of special significance, because women survive their husbands in increasing number. First, the average life expectancy of men is shorter than that of women, and, second, women generally marry men a few years their seniors. As medicine increasingly recognizes the special physical and emotional needs of old people, establishing a new medical specialty called "geriatrics," it will become more and more evident that women need to have a function as long as they live, which necessarily involves an ultimate functioning outside of the home.

The professional reorientation of women may well create more conflicts with husbands and with society as a whole. But the readjustment of all concerned is necessary to meet the problems of our present marriages as well as those of our changing society.

VIII.

PARENTHOOD

Can a marriage be complete without children? The answer to this question depends greatly on social conditions. Until recently, marriage without children was regarded as purposeless, as it still is among certain national and cultural groups. A marriage that remained childless lost its meaning and for that reason frequently could be dissolved. Mankind has, however, developed beyond this "naturalistic" view, for with the decrease in mortality of children and with the prolongation of human life, fertility has become less important for the preservation of mankind, nations, and races. General cultural and political conceptions determine the desire for children more than do economic necessities.

The relationship between economic conditions and the number of children is complex. Families who can afford many children generally have fewer than those who cannot afford them. Some couples plan parenthood in accordance with their ability to support children. Wanting children is natural, but social forces around us influence our

201

thinking so that we either procreate without restraint, or control our fertility even to the point of having no children.

PLANNED PARENTHOOD

The ability to conquer natural forces in the outside world and within himself enables man today to make a deliberate decision. We must recognize the antagonistic social tendencies which affect the individual and complicate the marital problems. On one side are certain religious and political demands to rear as many children as possible. The sociological background of the political encouragement of birth is obvious. Groups striving for national or racial superiority demand a large number of offspring to claim more rights and to supply armies to fight for them. It is more difficult to trace the social meaning of religious prescripts. The idea of Divine Providence excludes man's right to decide about life, which is given and taken by the Lord. A third factor responsible for large families today is quite different. It is indifference and ignorance which often prevent deliberate planning of parenthood.

On the other side we are confronted also by divergent forces coinciding in the demand for limited parenthood. A certain sense of responsibility prevents some married couples from having children, because they cannot offer what they feel children require—economic security, pleasant surroundings, a balanced and happy life, and reasonable prospects for the future. They question the right of anyone to produce children in times so distressing as the present. This argument in itself may be based on a real sense of responsibility and be part of an outlook on life following ideas of Malthus,[1] or it may express only personal cowardice and timidity. A more courageous person may see chances for progeny where a timid soul cannot envisage even his own survival. Selfish tendencies are frequently hidden behind a pretense of responsibility. Women may be more interested in "girlish figures" than in womanhood; men may consider the accumulation of money more important than spending it on children. Caring for a child may involve sacrifice of leisure time and freedom of movement.

The nature of the theses offered as reasons for or against procreation makes it difficult to decide in any one instance what influence the existence or nonexistence of children may have on the fate of the marriage. The outcome will depend very much on the moral forces involved. A couple having many children because they are inspired by deep religious feelings or by feelings of national and racial pride face different problems than a couple whose numerous offspring are the undesired products of carelessness or drunkenness. On the other side, a childless union as a result of selfishness and fear is different from the companionship of two people devoted exclusively to each other. Whether childbirth is avoided because of sincere consideration for the child or for consideration for the parents has practical consequences upon the marriage.

Since man has learned to regulate reproduction, there has been a definite tendency to reduce the number of offspring sharply. Moreover, the whole meaning of marriage has changed with the emancipation of women. Companionship has to a large degree replaced motherhood. Love has

[1] Thomas Robert Malthus, *An Essay on the Principle of Population.* J. Murray, London, 1817.

become meaningful even without "natural" consequences. Sexuality is no longer merely a scheming device of nature to force reproduction. Human sex proves thereby its independence of natural compulsion; it has changed its function from the animalistic drive as part of the reproduction process to a human practice for personal gratification. Love unites two human beings for common endeavor, and having children is only one part of their marital functions. Husband and wife have significance for each other apart from their potential parenthood.

THE FUNCTION OF CHILDREN

As before, however, parenthood today introduces a new element in an individual's life and changes his function distinctly. Once we are parents, each of us transcends the personal limitations of being an individual and expands self into an "I" which is self and still more than self. Parenthood further creates a feeling of unity between husband and wife unparalleled by any other experience of belonging together. Bringing a child into the world, if it is done deliberately and voluntarily, is one of the most complete expressions of social feeling—of feeling that we belong to the human community. It indicates the deep, unspoken acceptance of our obligation to give our best to mankind, and to human endeavor. Persons sensitive to duty and ready to accept particular responsibility for others rarely evade parenthood. A profound feeling for life, a deep interest in the future easily leads to the desire to bear children. For through our children we offer mankind something more than we ourselves are—the next generation.

There lies in human nature a desire to conquer death, a

longing for eternity that has found expression in the religious conceptions of resurrection and reincarnation. Likewise, in our work and in our contributions, our inventions and our creations, we try to survive spiritually—we long for immortality. In our children we actually become immortal. Very few realize the full implications of the desire to survive our own generation in our work, in our children. For survival through our work and our children means overcoming personal limitations. The more we free ourselves from physical limitations, the less we stress perpetuation of our own actual flesh and blood. Hence, our work, our progeny—and adopted children—serve a function: In them we survive spiritually, personally, as human individuals.

We must distinguish another motivation for having children. Sometimes parents want children in order to continue their own battles, to fulfill what they could not achieve for themselves. For them, children are not the expression of any feeling of belonging, of any social interest. Such parents do not want to contribute to mankind. They want only personal accomplices against "fate," against "the world." And their relationship to their children reflects their hostilities. They are incapable of recognizing their children as independent human beings. Unless the children surrender completely and accept their role as extension of parental ambition and desires, they have no meaning for the parents. In a similar position are children who are regarded by parents as precious substitutes for dogs or other pets, who exist merely to satisfy a flattering sense of superiority, personal vanity, or sensuous gratification.

For parents who recognize children as independent human beings, not here merely for the benefit of their parents, children are an inexhaustible source of pleasure and satisfaction so long as they are treated and cared for adequately. The life of a parent is richer, his interest generally broader than that of the childless man or woman. This, of course, is true provided the parent does not become the slave of the child whom he, for his own personal gratification, has made a god. But parenthood changes men. Previously interested exclusively in his job, in movies, bars, or gambling, a parent may discover the importance of civic institutions, public health regulations, and educational facilities. Moreover, a parent who shares the experiences of his children will attain something of their youth and himself remain young, again provided he is not in competition with his child, for then he may soon come to resent his child's age, which makes him old; mothers often are especially sensitive in this respect.

In evaluating the function of children in the marriage we must keep in mind the old truth that everything can be used for good or for ill. A child can be a link between husband and wife, or he can become a source of disunity. It all depends on whether they regard him as a common treasure or a bone of contention for each to claim. A child creates a great deal of responsibility. Rearing children is a very difficult task, and it is convenient to shift responsibility and blame. We must recognize all the obstacles which stand in the way of sharing and cooperating when faced with the difficulties inevitable in rearing children. If both parents realize the dictum: "These are *our* problems," if both parents are united in the rearing of a child, then they discover the great significance which the child has for their marriage, and they recognize a deeper purpose in being married.

206

Only in that way is it possible to derive profound satisfaction, more than compensating for all the unavoidable dangers and worries.

Certain problems of parenthood are peculiar to our times alone. Large families, which were once the rule, are uncommon. Especially in cities the average family has one or two children, seldom three, and rarely more. In these smaller families parents find it difficult to educate their children adequately and accomplish their social adjustment. In large families children grew up in a natural group, influencing each other; mother had no time for one in particular. She had to establish general rules for all her children. But in smaller families, children are much more exposed to their parents. An inadequate technique or attitude of a parent has far-reaching consequences, as there is nothing in the family to compensate for parental educational deficiencies.[2]

THE FUNCTION OF FATHER

Before we discuss the problems of education within the family, we must clarify the particular influence of the father and mother. The importance of the fact that parents belong to both sexes has previously been stressed. (Page 54).

The father plays a specific role in a child's education. He is the exemplum of what a man should be in life. The position of a man in the family largely depends on the cultural pattern prevailing in the particular family. In groups where the man is considered dominant, the father represents

[2] "The home is the original and most important breeding ground of courage to try and to learn from defeats, objectivity of viewpoint, and cooperation." N. E. Shoobs and G. Goldberg, *Corrective Treatment for Maladjusted Children.* Harper & Brothers, New York, 1942.

power and right. For children of such a father, man is definitely endowed with force, efficiency, and strength. This picture of a man, although abandoned in many American homes, is still prevalent in most parts of the world today. The picture of the dominant male is accentuated by the fact that in our culture man generally has a louder voice and as a rule is taller, because women generally select a mate taller and stronger than themselves. It also is generally the man who earns the money, a fact which gives him certain rights and makes him also the symbol of usefulness. As the father is generally engaged in work and business, his word and judgment mean encouragement or discouragement for his children in respect to work and business, or the equivalent of these. The limited amount of time which a working father can spend in the company of his children does not diminish but rather enhances his importance; children look forward to those few moments they can spend with their father. They will take his advice, his opinions, his suggestions very seriously so long as they are not set against him by their mother.

Despite these obvious paternal influences, men generally feel that they should not interfere in the education of their children. They consider it the special task of the mother. This abstinence has various psychological reasons. First, we may say that it is rarely a sincere respect for the mother's ability to perform the task adequately. Although fathers very often have a sense of inadequacy in regard to rearing children, they are also suspicious of the mother's ability. Their abstinence is a device by which they let her make mistakes and reserve for themselves the right to put full blame for any disturbance upon the mother. A second

208

reason for men's abstinence is the fear of being rebuked, of being told that they know nothing about education. It is not necessarily true that their wives know more. It cannot be denied that the mother, who spends more time with the children and must take care of them, is the most important factor in their lives but this explains rather than justifies the aloofness of many fathers. The child needs the influence of the father. Any father concerned more with the welfare of his child than with his own prestige will find a way to help the mother in the difficult task of rearing children.

THE FUNCTION OF MOTHER

The function of the mother remains almost the same under the various cultural patterns. If the natural closeness between mother and child is disturbed, the individual mother is responsible and not an external cultural or economic condition. For, normally, the mother is the first person concerned with and occupied with a newborn child: she nurtures it carefully and spends the first few weeks close to the child, gratifying his imperative needs. Whatever the child does is of utmost importance to her.

Their early training, through play (dolls, house) and indoctrination, provides women in general with an attitude, the so-called maternal instinct, which stimulates women to assume, wherever possible, a motherly role. If she fully utilizes her natural opportunities and is not in opposition to her feminine role, the mother should always find it easy to establish an intimate contact with the child. Every child has a tendency to lean a little more toward the mother as long as the mother does not disturb this natural development. Even if the mother has only limited time for the child, she can maintain this relationship. It is far less the amount of time which counts than how constructively it is used. Nothing can interfere with her influence if she is capable of being a good friend to her child, if she is willing to understand him, if she stands at his side as a staunch and loyal comrade. A child has a high regard for his mother if she has shown her ability to love him through all circumstances and despite all disappointments.

THE INADEQUACIES OF MOTHERS

This ideal of a mother, praised and sung with so much enthusiasm by poets and artists, contrasts sharply with the experiences that psychiatrists and educators have with mothers today. In appalling numbers we find mothers the source of the child's maladjustment and misery. The exercise of mother love under our present culture seems to be a task demanding almost superhuman qualities. Mother love, far from being the blessed thing pictured in old poems, turns too often rather into a weapon of evil. Under the name and pretense of mother love, a discouraged and rebellious, frustrated and antagonistic woman may demand praise for what is actually selfishness, fear, and domineeringness.

Yet there is no sense in blaming our mothers, because they are themselves victims. Women today face a struggle for their rights. They fear being the inferior sex. They are deeply disappointed in their relationships to men, in their marital experiences. For women have yet to win a place in our culture compatible with their talents and abilities. It is simply not true that women as a whole are not "mature," are emotionally unstable, are mentally or morally infantile or underdeveloped in comparison with men. What is sometimes described as feminine inability to think in abstract terms is actually a predilection for the functional; women have a particular sense for usefulness, acquired from generations spent under conditions which limited their activities as the inferior sex and demanded usefulness from them in the service of men. As a consequence, women as a whole (as far as generalities are permitted at all) are more inclined to sense real values, and fall less easily prey to imaginative and frequently dangerous fictions which often victimize the best masculine minds. Why then do so many women fail as mothers so much more frequently today than a few generations ago?

In a disturbed relationship between mother and child, the corruption of all human relationships becomes visible. Human beings today make very little preparation for harmonious cooperation. We need not be surprised to find that increasingly fewer women are prepared for the role of motherhood, which demands fully developed social interest.

A mother who is more interested in herself than in her child can never be a good mother. The deep love and affection which such a mother feels for the child is actually less concerned with the welfare and the development of the child than with her own satisfaction which she expects and demands. A child can give meaning to a marriage, which involves the relationship of several persons, but it can never be asked to provide meaning to one person's life. Yet just that is what some women, disappointed with life and somewhat estranged from their husbands, expect of their children. They want their children to belong to them and to be the purpose and meaning of their otherwise empty lives. Is this attitude love? Not at all. It is a compensation for uselessness. It is a demand for service.

Such a woman has not yet found her own place in the community. She may believe that she lives only for the child, but actually the child has to replace all other obligations which she would have to meet. Social contact, work, and the opposite sex become meaningless through this peculiar kind of "love." How many women regard their children as an increase to their glory—an additional rung in the ladder of their prestige! Some try to attract with their children the attention and admiration which other women receive for their legs. In more serious cases, the child has to provide an object for domination. He must fit, and often enough is brought up to fit into the personal life style of the mother. He is impressed with the danger of life, against which only mother love can give protection. By instilling fears and exercising domination under the pretext of an emotion which the mother, without any justification, calls "love," she begins a process of pampering and spoiling to bring the child under complete control and make him utterly dependent on her. In her own insecurity and distrust, she wants to be the only person trusted.

For a period of time, the child may find this overprotection agreeable, but sooner or later, the conflict begins. It may start, for example, when the second child is born and the mother becomes preoccupied with the baby. The first child feels deprived of the attention which previously had been showered on him. If the tragedy does not start then, the conflict is unavoidable when the child must go to school, when he must meet children of his own age. Fortunately, our present school system offers much help for pampered children in adjusting them to the social atmosphere and developing courage, independence, and social feeling. But all that does not solve the conflict with the mother. She either succeeds in keeping him close to her—then he never becomes adjusted to the group—or the child gains independence, and the fear and dominance of the mother expresses itself in open hostilities.

COMMON MISTAKES IN REARING CHILDREN

Indulging and pampering a child can never prevent friction but always lead to warfare. Underneath and beside the display of love and tenderness, we can always find expression of open or concealed hostility. Very few of these "loving" parents recognize the hostility and terrific warfare in which they and their children are involved. All the behavior problems of children are symptoms of hostility. It is difficult to make a mother aware of this. She cannot understand that the child may resent her, as she is firmly convinced that she gives him everything and loves him deeply. Yet how many mothers break down when they can no longer prevent the child from gaining independence? How many tragedies occur, especially during adolescence, when the child must grow up or become a complete failure—one being as distasteful to the mother as the other.

In protecting and dominating the child, not only mothers but many fathers try to prove their own superiority which is so badly threatened by our present life conditions. Once hostility starts, there is no relaxation, no peace. In a family shaken by discord and mutual hostility, shortcomings of the children are emphasized and actually fostered. Chil-

213

dren's faults serve as the basis of mutual recrimination, as opportunities for each parent to excuse his or her own lack of social adjustment, and for pretexts to justify their own expressions of hostility. The hostility may even start as soon as the child is born, without any original period of love and affection. Fortunately, complete rejection of children occurs less and less frequently since man has learned to prevent undesired offspring. In any case, the friction between parents and children, the warfare inside of the family, deprives many parents of the full gratification of having children.

It is no wonder that parents so often fail in the rearing of their children, for it is one of the most difficult tasks in marital life. Teaching is an art. It needs skills in which its practitioners must be carefully trained. But how much training do parents have? What do they know about education? The situation is the worse because what little they know is very often wrong and even harmful. No shoemaker would venture to open a shoe repair shop without being duly trained. But parents often open an educational workshop with almost no preparation—with only the training that they have received from their own parents.

Ironically, parents try to imitate the acts of their parents, completely forgetting what they themselves as children had to suffer from their own parents' inadequacy. A father who has been beaten as a child will be much inclined to beat his own children. He forgets completely the humiliation he felt as a child, the hatred and opposition growing under the whipping with the parental hand or rod. This is the reason why it is difficult to convince parents that their procedures and techniques are wrong, unsuccessful, or even harmful. Each parent represents in his attitude generations

214

whom he imitates. Any attempt to influence the educational procedure characteristic for any specific family is confronted with this unbreakable wall of traditional educational conceptions which are carried from one generation to another. This spiritual heritage is even stronger and more decisive than any physical inheritance. It may well be possible that certain national or racial characteristics are based less on biologically inherited qualities than on the educational methods used in the particular group and handed down from generation to generation.

To break this traditional circle is difficult indeed. Let us consider the simple traditional device of beating a child who deviates from the behavior desired by adults—who does "something wrong." What is the effect on the child? These cruel and terrifying episodes distort character, create a disbelief in human kindness and fellowship and a distrust of his fellows. Beaten children, in their revolt, provoke situations where they will be whipped again, physically as well as mentally. If, on the other hand, the spanked child keeps up courage and social interest, he will, as an adult, carefully avoid any situation in which he may be victimized again. He may cultivate "strength" and "toughness," and attain that rigidity and cruelty of character which is the high price paid by many strong and able persons. They punish rather than submit; and they alienate the affection of friends, relatives, and children.

Yet the custom of spanking was for a long time universally considered an adequate method of training children and still is accepted as such by most parents. Even those who recognize intellectually that spanking means humiliation and violation of human dignity, resort to this insulting technique for the preservation of their own superiority and excuse the practice by reference to their "uncontrollable" emotions and "nervous distress." The custom of spanking is one of the most forceful obstacles in the development of a democratic, peaceful, and cooperative atmosphere within the family, a relic of times which had little conception of human dignity and of human rights.

The problem of educating is not distinct from other problems of living together. The process of educating reveals one's general outlook, one's philosophy of life. The social atmosphere in a family is, therefore, a very important factor in the education of children. All the shortcomings, faults, and errors of a child can be traced to faulty approaches used by members of the family in dealing with each other. The child is adequately prepared for life only if the family has observed those rules which should govern the relations between human beings. For since the family is the child's first community and social unit, it represents to him a picture of life in general, and all depends on how closely and truthfully the family pictures the larger world outside. A favorable home atmosphere will encourage the development of a correct attitude in the child who, when he faces the world, must interpret it in accordance with the experiences and conceptions he has gained at home.

Unfortunately, the relationships within our present-day family do not correspond to those in life outside. Our children, especially if they are few, are usually overprotected, and they become self-centered. In a world of grown-ups, they live not as equals, but as dependents. They have few opportunities to become useful, to contribute to the group, and to achieve a proper niche by themselves. Their way of seeking the assurance of being accepted is demanding—demanding service from others, demanding gifts, or at least attention. What they can *receive* is for them a symbol of their importance; what they can *do* is insignificant. This principle of getting along with people contradicts all the rules of cooperation discussed earlier.

The more parents behave in accordance with the rules of cooperation, the easier it is for them to bring up their children properly. The child can adjust himself spontaneously to the right way of behavior, for he has a keen apprehension of what goes on around him, and how one must conduct himself to get along. Too often parents employ one set of rules for themselves and another, quite different, for their children. What excitement there is if a child lies! The parents are bewildered, they feel actually insulted. They completely forget the occasions when they have lied openly to a neighbor, or even demanded of the child that he lie for them. They expect their child to be industrious, whereas the father and the mother regularly complain about their own work. They are surprised by "improper" language from their child and ask accusingly where he learned to speak thus, when the child is merely repeating what he has heard from them. Is it so foolish for a child to say to his mother, "If you are not nice to me, I won't clean my room," if the mother demands that the child be "nice" before she fulfills her own obligation to the child? Yet the demanding mother is horrified by such statements.

It is difficult for parents to realize that children are human beings like themselves. Parents not only demand privileges which disrupt social order and destroy the feeling of belonging; but often they permit the child privileges that they would not grant to anyone else. Indulgence is as disastrous as suppression. Only rules which govern the life of the whole family, which include parents and children alike, train for the recognition of right and wrong. Where strong and impartial moral rules regulate the family life, no particular educational techniques are required for the child to grow up willing to contribute his share, confident of his own strength and ability, a useful vital force in the community at large.

Where is there a family with such background and atmosphere? Where are there parents so courageous and cooperative? As has been mentioned, our times are unfavorable to the development of such a family and such parents. A deep feeling of insecurity and a constant concern regarding our prestige hinders us from being as good human beings as we could be. Parents are no exception.

We cannot expect parents to be more cooperative with their children than they are with other competitors. And it is as foolish to expect more peace within the family than within our society as a whole. With sufficient social feeling, we find our way everywhere—without it, nowhere. Children are not different from other human beings. They can threaten the prestige of their parents as much as business competitors, perhaps even more; for parents are very vulnerable to their children's opposition. They believe that parental love or parental indulgence can buy submission. They demand acceptance and obedience just because they are parents. Any opposition and disobedience they regard as a personal affront, almost as a heinous sacrilege against the "divine idea of parenthood." The more they try to impose their will upon the child, the less they succeed in winning his cooperation, and their sense of disappointment deepens. Chagrined and embittered by life, they take their disappointment home and return it through their children back to the world.

PROPER METHODS OF HANDLING CHILDREN

It becomes necessary, then, to formulate some principles for influencing children. Parents need advice, because the pattern of their lives does not guarantee the wholesome development of the child. It is impossible here to discuss in detail the methods of home education. The few principles in the chapter on "Living Together," however, offer a wide range of adequate approaches. The first underlying principle is the comprehension of and respect for human dignity. In dealing with a child, adults must respect their own dignity, and also that of the child. Neglecting one's own dignity means indulgence; neglecting the child's dignity is suppression. Both destroy cooperation, both establish tyrants and slaves.

Another principle is: "Neither fight nor give in." For the purpose of family education, one must add the postulates, "Win the child to an acceptance of order" and "Encourage the child." These three principles, no fighting, maintaining order, and giving constant encouragement, belong intrinsically together. No one is possible without the other two. If we fight, we shall never be capable of making the child accept order and invariably will discourage the child. Failing to insist that the child observe order leads inevitably to fighting; a child will not be able to conform to order and will force his parents to fight him.

219

For many parents, it is impossible to believe that children can be brought up without being subjected to force. "Spare the rod and spoil the child" is a characteristic expression of distrust in human nature, which, in this view, can best be tamed, but never made social without coercion. Such parents need to be convinced that when they resort to fighting the child, they are inevitably the losers. The child has too many advantages in his favor—he knows so much better how to handle his parents than they know how to treat him. Devoting all his time to observing his environment, he knows each parent's vulnerable spot. He is imaginative and invents hundreds of modes of warfare, while the rigid adult sticks to three or four measures which, in addition, are mostly ineffectual. The child knows exactly how to get his way, and the parents, despite all fighting, inevitably yield.

It becomes obvious that fighting is useless. All the methods of humiliation—shouting, scolding, and spanking—succeed only for the moment, if they have any effect at all. The child strikes back at the first opportune occasion, and for each apparent victory of the parents the child scores at least ten real victories. Habitual disobedience is a natural consequence. But where there is a friendly relationship with a real understanding between parents and child, how easy things are! Every child is very sensitive to kindness—and to firmness, too. Children who do not respond have been taught that only force is important.

Mary was playing in the yard when Mother called, "Mary, come here." Continuing her play, Mary showed no signs of having heard. Mother called again. And again there was no response. A family friend passing by listened to Mother's call several times, then approached Mary and asked her whether she had not heard the call. "Oh, yes!" she replied quietly, continuing her play. The friend was a little indignant. "Then why don't you go home?" Undisturbed, Mary answered, "Oh, I have time. Mother hasn't yelled yet!"

Many parents—and the best ones—fail woefully to recognize the importance of order. They sincerely love the child. They want to save him any disappointment or painful experience. Because they want to make his life happy, they eliminate any rule of order. The child's wish is their command. They hope that later on the child will learn to understand better and be more sensibly inclined. How wrong they are! Once a child has learned that his desire is omnipotent, he must regard any attempt to deny his omnipotence, whether of parents or teachers, as an injustice, as an effort to deprive him of privileges he considers his natural right, and will interpret it as a sign of rejection and humiliation. Overprotection and indulgence never win a child, never make him cooperative and courageous. They deprive him of enjoying order, of experiencing his own strength in helping himself and being useful to others. Instead of preventing unpleasant experiences, indulgence exposes the child to more and worse suffering. Instead of helping him, it endangers him; and the fight and friction, always dreaded, become inevitable.

Indulgence is often based on a faulty idea of freedom. To give children freedom and self-expression is necessary; but freedom without order is impossible. On the other hand, there is no permanent order without freedom. In some cultures, the idea of order is exaggerated to such an extent that children are deprived of any self-expression. Strict

221

rule and instant obedience are the main goals of education. The consequences are identical with those produced by suppression and humiliation. Toughness, strength, and success may be achieved in that way, but the human relationship suffers. On the other hand, this very human relationship is endangered just as much by another frequent misunderstanding of freedom. Freedom is not the right to do whatever we want, because such freedom necessarily means imposition on others to whom we then deny the same privilege. If everyone acts as he likes, disregarding the desires of his fellow men, then no one can enjoy freedom—only anarchy results. Freedom and special privilege for one person cannot be called freedom at all. It is actually tyranny and dictatorship. Under the pretext of granting freedom parents make their children unhappy despots who are unable to get along with others and feel rejected by everyone not submissive to their rule.

Many children grow up with a very peculiar conception of order. For them order is everything that they don't want to do. They must learn to recognize that order is beneficial to them. It is not at all difficult to teach them this. When a child refuses to submit to the routine which regulates the life of the family, we can help him to understand better what order means. There are many ways to impress a child with the real significance of order. For example, he may agree that it would be nice if each member of the family could do—for a day or so—whatever he likes best. Very soon, the child will discover that he gains very little and loses very much if father and mother also do only what they like best at any given moment. There are no meals prepared, no beds made, and no clothes cleaned. Obviously order serves not the interest of any one person but all of them together. Freedom is only the liberty of acting independently as long as one does not infringe upon the freedom of anyone else.

And now the third and most important rule: The child needs constant encouragement. He needs encouragement as a plant needs water. Our present method of rearing children is instead full of discouragement. Indulgence and suppression create innumerable experiences of discouragement. For parents are needlessly timid. They see everywhere possible dangers; they identify themselves with their children, and, having no confidence in themselves, they can hardly believe that the child can take care of himself. Instead of recognizing the potentialities of a child, they compare his size and capacity with their own and conclude that he must be so many times less capable than they themselves are. In reality, the child generally has more physical and mental abilities than the parents credit him with. This doubt in the child's potentialities, carried from one generation into the next, is one of the reasons why adults leave so many of their capacities undeveloped, never reaching the fruition of their potentialities.

Any educational procedure may best be evaluated according to the degree of encouragement it involves. Whatever increases the courage of a child is helpful—and whatever discourages, harmful. No child is genuinely "bad." Every child likes to be good, wishes to be successful, loves to be "nice." Only if he gives up hope, if he loses confidence in himself, only then will he misbehave. The technique of encouragement is not yet fully recognized and fostered. Very few people deliberately plan to encourage, and even those frequently don't know how. Some try to be sweet—how the children hate that! Children observe very closely—too closely not to recognize insincerity. Dishonest praise can never encourage. Undeserved commendation is either meaningless or disgusting. Even sincerely expressed admiration may discourage a child, despite his pleasure in it, if he feels that he cannot live up to the high appreciation.

These two factors seem to be essential for encouragement: sincerity and recognition of the personal needs of the child. Each child has abilities and faculties which can be commended, and each has sore spots which need tender care. Without having faith in the child, however, no one will be able to instill in him a better opinion of himself. Self-confidence, recognition of the strength of his own faculties, means courage. Whosoever can provide it can enhance the efficiency and facilitate necessary social adjustments of any person he meets—especially of a child yearning for just this kind of assistance.

Influences that encourage, natural in a friendly atmosphere, are impossible where antagonism reigns, where hostility, non-compliance, and mutual depreciation dominate the human relationship. When husband and wife disagree, when parents fight with each other, then the children, too, compete with each other, each one trying to dishearten his adversary of the moment. How many and how subtle are the means by which parents stifle their child's natural and diversified talents, discourage his efforts, and prevent the development of his feeling of confidence in his own value and in his creative power.

Every mistake and every fault in a child reflects the discouragement to which he has been exposed in his family.

Otherwise, he would have found a better answer to his problem. A child brought up in an atmosphere of love and understanding is eager and willing to do his share. Surrounded by friendliness and genuine interest, he develops happily and responds to the social demands. But as so many parents and teachers themselves are the product of an atmosphere of friction and competition, they fail to provide proper guidance to the child. They forget the terrible feeling of insecurity, of detachment, of being unloved, which they probably experienced themselves. They learn less from studying child psychology than from their own unbringing. Far from discovering the child's possibilities, they oppose what he does, they hinder him, but hardly stimulate him. Yes, sometimes they achieve obedience, but at what price? They have in their efforts ruined a personality. They do not understand why a child feels neglected—they are completely unaware of why he behaves disturbingly.

UNDERSTANDING THE CHILD

To understand a child one needs full knowledge of the reasons for his development. Many of his traits are due to his trying to find his position in the family group, or seeking methods which bring recognition and which prove to be effective in the particular setting of his environment. Without encouragement and guidance, the child fails time and again in finding socially accepted methods of dealing with others. Misbehavior and disturbance result.

Four main objectives can be discerned as motivating a child to misbehave. We must understand these goals before we can hope to change the child's behavior.

Most frequently, the child wants to attract attention.

This particular desire prevails in younger children. In the family situation of today, children have little opportunity to be useful, to gain social recognition by contributing to the common goal. They, therefore, come to believe in the importance of receiving—gifts, affection, or at least attention. The toy which father brings home is less desirable as a tool of enjoyment than as a token of father's love. Devoid of attention, the child feels neglected. If he cannot obtain attention in a pleasant way, he turns to disagreeable ways and deliberately provokes scolding and punishment. That at least is attention; remaining unnoticed is worse. Not even to be punished is complete rejection; worst of all is to be ignored. Children who strive for attention must be taught that they can be useful—that social recognition means not receiving, but contributing.

The second possible objective of any disturbance is to demonstrate superiority and power. Children exposed to force learn to counteract with resistance. The more one demands of them, the less they conform. Children are very ingenious in frustrating the most forceful schemings of their parents, and gain easy victories while their adversaries are bewildered and dumbfounded.

This hostility leads finally to the third objective, namely, to punish, to get even. Convinced that nobody likes him, the child gives up any attempt to please. The only compensation for his humiliation is his ability to hurt others as he is hurt. No sense of social responsibility impedes his desire to take for himself whatever seems gratifying. This aggressive behavior expresses complete social discouragement.

The fourth objective is evidenced in complete passivity.

It expresses a belief in personal inadequacy. It is an attempt to avoid situations where the anticipated personal deficiency would become obvious.

To comprehend malfunctions we must know which one of these four goals is behind them. Many believe they understand a certain behavior if they find a word adequate to describe it. But words don't explain qualities, they only describe them. The word laziness, for instance, does not explain a definite behavior; psychologically each example of laziness differs from others. One child is lazy in order to get attention—mother must sit near by to remind and help; otherwise, the homework won't be done. But laziness can mean superiority and power; against all threats and punishments of parent or teacher, the child flatly refuses to work. Sometimes laziness is the worst revenge of a mishandled child—punishing vain and over-ambitious parents. In many cases laziness means just the discouraged attitude of giving up. What is the sense of trying if one cannot hope to make the grade anyhow?

Parents must learn to understand such tendencies—they must know why the child behaves as he does; against whom and what he directs his aggression or shortcomings. They should know more—although they rarely do. Parents should gather information about the general line of the child's thoughts and desires, about his conception of life and of himself, about his attempts and the conclusions he draws from his experiences.

THE LIFE STYLE

Under the influence of all his experiences, the child develops rather early—within the first four to six years of his

227

life—a definite idea of himself and of his position in life. According to his interpretation of observations and his understanding of social living he develops certain approaches to the social problems of life, being stimulated by guiding lines offered through actions and successes and failures observed in parents and siblings. Each individual develops characteristic approaches which form the basis of his unique personality. He may change his techniques according to the situation which he encounters; but the basic idea of himself remains the same. If a child comes to the conclusion that he always needs others to depend upon, then he naturally will behave differently when he finds such support than when he lacks it. In the first instance he may be very cooperative and apparently well adjusted; while he will fail or withdraw if he is left to his own resources. The reason behind these two contradictory behavior patterns is identical.

The child is not aware of his own concepts but responds to their disclosure. If they are not made clear to him he carries his mistaken concepts into grown-up life and can only change them for a better orientation through psychotherapy. Parents who are trained in recognizing the basic ideas of their child can help a great deal to prevent the formation of misconceptions which may later lead to social maladjustment, failure, and unhappiness.

THE FAMILY CONSTELLATION

The concepts of a child are very much influenced by his position in the family. In the life of an only child, the parents are the most important figures during his first decisive years of life. The parents' reaction to the child's experimental efforts in dealing with them regulates the child's behavior, although not always in a desired and desirable fashion, because the child's idea of success does not always correspond with the parents'. He may think that they must serve him. Furthermore, the parents' personalities and their own behavior offer the child guiding lines in developing his own approaches; judging again from his own point of view, he adopts the methods and the behavior he considers effective.

Unfortunately, again his opinion does not always coincide with his parents' as, for instance, when he finds that being afraid gets him special consideration. When the child has brothers and sisters, however, they generally become more important for his development than the parents, who then assume the role of moderators, accentuating and managing the position which each child occupies in the group. By emphasizing particular traits and abilities in each child, they play a part in the existing competition between the children, and are very often the power behind the scenes, unaware of pulling the strings, and bewildered by the results. The competition between brothers and sisters is one of the strongest influences in the development of every child. Its results are obvious, even if the children are devoted to each other and do not fight and quarrel openly. Signs of competition can easily be recognized, if one is acquainted with them.

The competition among siblings starts with the peculiar relationship between the first and second child. The basic element for the maintenance of competition is provided by the child's inability to comprehend the importance of age. For a child, his brother or sister is simply stronger or weaker, more or less capable, irrespective of his age. Parents' soothing references to changing age—"You will be able to do that, too, when you're older"—are meaningless to the child. In two years he will be able to do what his older brother can do today; but, by that time, the older brother is again—or still—two years ahead. These two years make all the difference, not as years, but through their consequences in regard to difference in size, in power, in skill, in faculty. Age, as such, becomes a factor when used to play one child against the other. The degree of seniority is irrelevant. We have seen children whose seniority privileges were actually based on a very short time-interval. In some of my cases only seven or thirteen minutes made all the difference, qualifying one as the older with definite privileges of seniority.

Because the competition between the first child and the second is almost universal, such children offer the best demonstration of its significance. The first, having been for a time the only child, regards the second as threatening his privileged position. He finds himself compelled to share not only the time and attention, but also the affection of his parents, especially of his mother. The birth of a sibling is always a shock to an only child, who usually feels "dethroned." Even if he has been prepared for this event, he can hardly foresee the implications of a situation never experienced before. In the best case, he is sufficiently assured of his superiority as an older child, and may be willing to accept the coming of a playmate as rescue from isolation, splendid though it might have been.

Usually, however, the first-born watches with growing apprehension the development of the new-born baby. He

230

perceives that his advantages in ability and functioning, tremendous at the outset, decrease with each month and year. He must fear the moment when the newcomer will be equal to him, because then it would take only one step further and the second one would be ahead of him. This fear generally materializes sooner than he anticipates. Parents not fully aware of this conflict foolishly play the younger against the elder, and thereby intensify the natural competition with disastrous results. When the child employs disturbing behavior to attract the attention previously exclusively his, parents become indignant; their delight with the charming little baby contrasts sharply with their display of disgust and annoyance at the older child, proving to him how justified his fears are.

The predicament of the older child is further complicated by the younger one's natural desire to compensate for his own difficulty. He constantly has another child ahead of him, who can walk, talk, manage himself, go to school, read and write, whereas he cannot. Isn't it only natural that he tries with all his force to strengthen his position? As soon as the second child discovers any shortcomings in his senior, he grasps this opportunity. Mother's casual remark that the elder one might take an example from the younger's cleanliness offers such an opportunity: now the second one can excel. The older, in turn, fully recognizes the danger. Far from improving, as his mother had hoped he would, he is inclined to give up. His little brother, so much smaller and so much inferior, can do something better than he can. What's the use of trying any more?

This is a typical situation: One child, discouraged by the success of another, decides unconsciously that his strength lies somewhere else, leaving this particular field to the more successful competitor. Once the idea has taken root, a vicious circle ensues. The more one child gives up, the more the other one tries to establish his own superiority in this particular field, and the more successful he is, the less hope the other entertains. The green light for one is the red light for the other. And the parents, instead of breaking the vicious circle while it still is easily possible, intensify it by siding with the more successful child. The two children divide the world between them—where one may rely on his intelligence, the other one may develop his charm. If one is interested in studies, the other one seeks to excel in athletics. One is good in languages, therefore the other one is more interested in mathematics. One is reliable and dependable; the other becomes helpless and dependent. If one is exceptionally well behaved we can always look for his competitor, who pays the price. Success can be achieved by either the first or the second child—conditions and attitudes of the parents decide the outcome. Generally, the more pampered or suppressed one child is, the better chances has the other. In most cases, the chances are somewhat divided, so that neither fails nor succeeds completely in every regard. Under fortunate conditions, the competition may not lead to failure in any sense, but rather to successes in contrasting fields.

The following case shows very clearly the mechanisms and the expressions of competition between children.

Nine-year-old Billy was such a wonderful little boy. He had lost his father four years ago, and he managed to be a great solace and help to his mother. Very early he assisted her not only in housework, but also in taking care of six-year-old

Marilyn. Even at his tender age, Mother could discuss any problem with him, and he actually assumed the function of the "man of the family." The only point where Billy did not do so well was at school. He had few friends and was not very much interested in school work. That is not surprising when we consider that in school Billy could not have the extraordinary position which he enjoyed at home.

One can easily imagine the type of girl Marilyn was. She was so unruly that Mother did not know what to do with her any longer and asked for help. She was untidy, unreliable, noisy, disturbing, and annoying—a real "brat." Mother could not understand how in all the world the two children could be so different! It was hard for her to understand the connection between Billy's goodness and Marilyn's difficulties.

We had the following discussion with both children together. First, we asked Marilyn whether she thought Mother liked her. Her answer was, as could be expected, a shaking of the head. Then we explained to her that we were sure that Mother loved her very much but that because she, Marilyn, did not believe it, she acted in such a way as to make Mother constantly angry at her. As a consequence, Mother paid attention to her only when she misbehaved (destructive attention-getting mechanism) and that made her feel still more disliked. If she would try to behave differently, she would find out that Mother loved her, too.

This discussion took place in the presence of Billy. Then we asked him whether he wanted Marilyn to be a good and nice girl. He immediately shouted, "No!" We asked him why he didn't want it. He became embarrassed, groped for some answers, and finally said, "She won't be good, anyhow." Then we explained to him that maybe we could help her and he could help her, too, and so we might succeed in making her a good girl. Would he like it? Somewhat uncertainly, he said, yes, he would like it. I looked at him and told him, frankly, I didn't believe that he meant it seriously; I was sure that his first "no" was more sincere and accurate. But why didn't he want her to be good? Perhaps he could tell me. He was thoughtful for a while. And then he came out—"Because I want to be better."

Once the competition between the first and second child is established, a third child may be adopted as an ally by either the first or the second. Only rarely does the third compete with both, forcing the first and second into an alliance with each other—a situation which may occur, for example, if the older two are girls and the youngest a boy. The fourth one can side with any of the older children, according to circumstances. Whichever way the division of forces have been aligned can be recognized easily by each child's subsequent character development. The two siblings most different in their qualities, interests, or emotions are those who as children were competitors. This fact reveals where within the family lie the battlefronts, the recognition of which is necessary for the understanding of any child.

This family interaction, which puts each child in a characteristic "family constellation" as Adler [3] calls it, is more important for the development of personality and character than any other single factor such as inheritance. Here is an example:

Father, mother, and six children make up the family. The competition originated in the relationship of a "superior," domineering father, interested in politics and literature, and the mother, a typical housewife, compensating for her social and intellectual inadequacy by domestic dominance over the children. The first child, Sally, a daughter, is played by her father against the mother. The mother finds an ally in her second daughter, Beatrice. Sally is a good student, but despises housework and is in constant opposition to her mother. Beatrice is very much interested in housework, a very mediocre student, and much interested in her feminine appeal.

A few years later identical twin girls are born. Their physical

[3] Alfred Adler, *Understanding Human Nature*. Greenberg Publishers, New York, 1927.

234

similarity necessitates their wearing different-colored stockings and ribbons to facilitate recognition. Identical twins generally have a peculiar psychological relationship. They identify themselves with each other to such a degree that very often they regard themselves as only a half of one, frequently developing identical life styles which then bring an amazing similarity in their fortunes.

In our case, however, something rather unusual happened. The strong competition between the two older sisters caused a division between the twins. One, Ruth, who was, incidentally, the senior by thirteen minutes, was claimed by Sally as an ally, while Beatrice sided with the "younger" twin, Diana. As a consequence, Ruth developed like Sally into a good student and bad housekeeper, while Diana, like Beatrice, became a mediocre student, good housekeeper, and much interested in her appearance. The third couple of children were a boy and a girl. The boy, Tom, was not only again the "older" of the two, but also, as a boy, desirous of special superiority.

The whole family was split into two groups—in character, in interests, and behavior: Father, Sally, Ruth, and the boy against Mother, Beatrice, Diana, and the baby girl. Tom, with the support of his oldest sister and father, challenged the superiority of even his much older sister, Beatrice, trying to bully her. The twin Ruth excluded Diana from her own relationship with girls, and refused to take her with them because she was "too young" (thirteen minutes younger!). Friction, discord, and mutual suffering made miserable the life of these otherwise capable and pleasant human beings.

ADJUSTING CHILDREN TO SOCIAL LIVING

Overcoming the spirit of competition within the family and especially between the children is one of the most difficult, yet most urgent tasks for conscientious parents. Just as this competition inhibits the children from enjoying each other, any experience of mutual enjoyment lessens the competition. What the family needs is united activity and common interests to increase this feeling of belonging together, which is the best antidote to segregation through competition. Games, which give everyone an equal and fair chance, tours and outings, alluring common interests, discussions inviting everyone to express his opinion, are extremely effective, especially if both parents participate. But without deliberate effort, real group activity will seldom develop: The games may sustain the competition by permitting to one child his customary superiority while assigning to the other his customary submissiveness. Although some kind of equilibrium always exists, it is not necessarily a happy one and if it is unhappy it can be definitely destructive psychologically. Each child should be trained for occasional leadership and for occasional submission if democratic ways are to develop within the family and thence extend to broader social groups.

One word as to the pressing problem of whether children should be saved from the "ugly" influences of the outside world. One hears persistently the cry, "Let's protect our children!" This demand is well intentioned but dangerous. Our children are protected too much anyhow. By protecting them we do not prepare them to face life later on. What they need is not protection, but encouragement. Let them face the facts of life squarely; one can't conceal them anyhow. But parents can help their children to develop a correct attitude toward life, to be courageous and sympathetic, understanding and helpful. Instead of forbidding children to listen to the horror stories of the radio, parents can help them to evaluate the stories correctly and to scorn what is just cheap and sensational. They can't successfully forbid their children to play with guns, if their playmates do so (by the way, playing with guns is not appropriate preparation for being a soldier and serves only to foster a misguided sense of superiority); but parents can teach their children the true meaning of gunplay. They can give them a better approach toward achieving superiority and demonstrating their own value.

Given this help, the child will become, in his group, a force of enlightenment. He will spread moral values which he learned from his parents. We cannot prevent our children's learning about the horrors of war, but we can discuss with them the ideals of democracy and liberty. We can make them understand that fighting is not an effective way for establishing superiority, but a necessary means of self-defense. The child can find adequate ways of dissolving friction and should be strong and self confident enough to resist aggression.

Interference by parents in the conflicts that children have with each other is mostly harmful. If the friction is within the family, the parents' meddling increases the competition and encourages only more fighting, which gives wonderful opportunities to evoke the parents' attention. If the fight is outside the family, parental influence helps little to lessen the tension and undermines the child's ability to take care of himself. In emergency, of course, educational considerations must be put aside in favor of safety. Such situations, however, are far less frequent than timid parents believe. If siblings quarrel, don't think that they will kill each other. I like to put two children who are fighting vigorously into a room by themselves, with the remark that I will see which one comes out alive. Usually that device helps. After a short while each child is sitting in a corner, or both are playing harmoniously together.

Yes, bringing up children is difficult. We know that we must have sympathy with parents. If there is only one child, he is in the difficult position of living among giants. If there are two children, strong competition develops and the children fight and quarrel. If there are three children, one is always the middle child, and, comparing his position with the privileges of the older and the younger one, he is inclined to feel neglected. If there are four children, we often find two antagonistic pairs of first and second children, but, as a rule, with four the situation improves considerably. But who can wait until he has four children?

Thus, we must have sympathy for the poor parents, or at least the poor mothers, because fathers tend to withdraw from a job which is often more difficult than their daily work. Parents are the real problem—not children. We must help them so that they will be able to enjoy the deepest pleasure human beings can experience—having children. Whoever learns to enjoy his child is glad to pay the price demanded—sleepless nights at the bedside of a sick child; fright and consternation at dangers; disappointments and concern when the child fails. Watching the child grow up is a pleasure unequaled. It reverses the meaning of time; every year lost to us is gained by the child. Our own stepping aside is more than compensated by our child's taking up where we leave off, not for our personal prestige, but for the maintenance of our ideals, of our convictions, of all that we consider worthwhile. Through our children we build the future, and the future alone can appraise what we do today.

IX.

SOLVING THE PUZZLE OF SEX

THE POWER OF THE INDIVIDUAL

FEW realize how their efforts to solve their personal problems of today stimulate an evolution which may eventually offer an adequate answer to many distressing puzzles of sexual and marital living. While we are fulfilling our daily tasks, trying to support ourselves, seeking love and getting married, enjoying friendships and participating in various activities, we may not be thinking about the future, but all that we are doing leads into the future—it makes the future. Each one of us helps mold the world of tomorrow. Every man and every woman, consciously or unconsciously, is vital for evolution. How ignorant most of us are of the tremendous strength and influence we individually wield! Many believe, curiously enough, that only politicians effect changes in the structure of our society. But, as a matter of fact, every human being, through his activity—and equally through his inactivity—actually effects the changes, whether he wills it or not. Every thought and every action, every belief and every doubt, every desire and every indifference—all are elements which weave themselves into

239

the intricate pattern of public opinion. Though they may lose individual distinction in the web, they color the fabric of our tomorrow.

Our thoughts and feelings about love and marriage are forces in the evolutionary process. The existence of conflicting opinions indicates the process of change. Our desire to recast and remold, or our placid contentment in the present conditions influence the development. How and when we fall in love, how we experience sex, whether we marry or not, how we live with our spouse, and what we think about divorce not only affects our own life but has significance for all our contemporaries. We reinforce certain social trends and negate others, while we believe that we are minding our own business. We need to become more aware of the part we play through our opinions in the concerted strivings of mankind toward a more satisfactory way of living. We must learn to evaluate better the social meaning of our personal convictions and preferences. The awareness of our own role can make us more deliberate in our intentions and help us understand those beliefs of our fellow men which contradict our own. Both an attitude of deliberation and an understanding of others are essential for a democratic integration of all our existing points of view into the one current of actual evolution.

But let us go back to the immediate problem of ourselves. We want to know what is right and what is wrong—what we should do or what we should avoid. For this reason alone it is necessary to have some understanding of the trends of development. Otherwise we remain helpless in the confusion of change and of contradicting values and morals. Let us discuss a few of the most disturbing problems and let us see in which direction the general development points.

THE CONFUSION OF SEX

There is first the problem of sexual activity, which arouses so much concern and discussion. No other problem of love and marriage provokes so much argument and difference of opinion. Some declare themselves openly in favor of sexual "freedom" for both men and women alike; some decry the new so-called immorality, and some avoid taking any definite stand, perhaps adhering by their practice to one point of view and by their convictions to the other. Many enjoy sexual freedom outside marriage and still speak about the sin of "fornication." Others fool themselves in the other direction. I heard one girl saying that she believed in free love but did not practice it. Confusion over confusion! What is right and what is wrong?

Why are all so much absorbed with sex? It seems to be a general rule that whenever we are confronted with some problem we feel unable to solve, it occupies us continually. Day and night (yes, in our dreams, too) we are beset by the persistent enigma of sex in all its physiological, human, and social aspects. We make a hundred unsuccessful attempts to solve it, and each failure magnifies the issue until its exaggerated proportions obliterate every other important phase of human relationships. And so sex becomes for many persons a symbol of life and its sole meaning. For all those discouraged in love, who have found themselves inadequate to establish a satisfactory and human relationship with the opposite sex, sex itself develops into some kind of mania. Their whole life perspective becomes awry.

Actually, sexuality is only one phase of the relationship between men and women. Those constantly concerned with sexual functions disregard the human aspect of the relationship and look upon persons of the opposite sex as objects or victims to be conquered, but hardly as human beings. Even if they do proceed to regard each other as potential husband or wife, we can often discover behind the sexual attraction the emerging picture of a potential enemy. The problem of sexuality becomes confused because so much emphasis is placed on the sexual expediency of a mate; and other capacities, abilities, and interests are either overlooked completely or given only secondary and incidental consideration.

Present conditions do not permit any humane quality to find its full expression. This is important, as all marital and sexual problems confronting individuals or couples depend on the conventions prevalent in their community. For this reason there is no generally accepted solution possible. Religious, national and cultural concepts decide, for instance, what constitutes sexual "decency." [1] In some communities intimate sexual relations have no legal or moral place outside the bounds of matrimony. In a community which considers the unwed mother a disgrace and ostracizes her and her "bastard," provisions to protect the interests of an illegitimate child will hardly be carried out.

On the other hand, we find groups and communities with a different point of view, generally called "liberal" or "modern." They must make some concessions to the law, to gen-

[1] "All standards of behavior are relative, depend on patterns of culture. Culture is local, manmade, and hugely variable." Ruth Benedict, *Patterns of Culture;* Houghton Mifflin Company, Boston, 1934.

erally accepted morals, but, far from scorning free love, they pride themselves in their sexual emancipation. One community does not object if an unmarried couple indulge in intimate relationship; another grants only the man the right of extramarital sex experiences; whereas a third condemns any sexual relationship out of wedlock. Although the decisive factor is the status of women in a particular society, we ourselves take part in establishing and maintaining the standard.

If a girl asks whether she should have sex relations with her fiancé, the prevailing conventions of the community and the attitude of both individuals toward emancipation must be considered. It is impossible to say yes or no, because either answer may imperil her future. The tradition in which the boy was reared must be considered as well as his personal development. Many a boy will not marry a girl after she has lost her virginity, although he may try his best to make her lose it. Yielding to such a man would mean losing him with the virginity. Some boys, however, will hesitate to marry unless they feel such closeness to the girl as is possible only through sex; such a boy may doubt being liked enough if the girl resists.

All those who object to such statements must recognize the problems of our youth. Our young people do not live under the conditions which existed when their parents grew up. If we want to help them and give them guidance and orientation, we must recognize the new social status of women and the different set of values and morals developed in the past twenty-five years. Our youngsters are not "immoral"; their morals are only different from those of the previous generations. The parents know it, but want to shut their eyes to new and disturbing facts. A mother realizes that her son cannot marry very young, and probably won't remain "chaste" until a mature age. She tries not to think about what he should do. Should he seek a "loose" girl or a "nice" one for his sexual experiences? Mothers of girls usually have different opinions than mothers of boys. Many girls don't know what to think, either. They want their husbands to have had experiences, but with whom? Here the thinking becomes confused. They don't like their future husbands to have had experiences with morally inferior women; yet they are "nice" girls and want to preserve their own chastity. Moreover, they resent his privilege in having sex experience. And so they are enmeshed in a struggle, a problem full of contradictions and entanglements. Their keen observation comes in conflict with religion and traditions. Their intellectual conclusions contradict their feelings, and even those intellectual recognitions are of questionable permanence.

This confusion characterizes a certain mental laziness of our present generation, which wants to abide by old traditions and at the same time satisfy new social demands. It leads to all the fallacies governing the love lives of a great many people. We believe in monogamy, and at the same time revolt against it, by longing for change and variety. We have a high regard for virginity, but do not esteem girls who have no virtues other than their "decency." Girls look for any kind of sexual gratification, but want to preserve their technical virginity. They all seek a solution without taking any stand. They want to accept and reject at the same time, and finally find that they can't fool anyone except themselves.

The conflicts arise from an incomplete recognition of one's own outlook and intentions. It is necessary to think through the problems involved and have the courage to abandon the past and step forward deliberately toward the goal desirable for mankind. Such thinking is a prerequisite to a clear stand, free from confusion and inner contradictions. We cannot expect mere instruction—moral, ethical, or even medical—to resolve our difficulties. What we need is a clear perception of the social issues at stake and the evolutionary effect of our course of conduct.

THE DIRECTION OF CHANGES

Since Plato's *Republic* and Sir Thomas More's *Utopia*, many visionary novels have been written visualizing a world with fundamentally different values and principles. Scientifically one cannot depict any detail of life under conditions completely foreign to our present social order. However, general trends of the past evolution indicate the direction of present developments.

Every war accelerates change. Tradition and routine, eternal opponents of progress, are swept away by the vital needs of self-defense. Latent social forces are suddenly released, and the solution of social problems, long postponed, becomes imperative. The First World War, which involved the whole civilian population far less than the second one, brought far-reaching social and economic changes, especially in Europe. It affected the position of women and brought them a status never previously experienced. The recent war is bound to further this development considerably. Women took men's places not only in industry, in commerce, in art, and in science, but even in the armed forces. This last is of tremendous significance, as membership in the armed forces has been for thousands of years the privilege of the dominant masculine sex. Women were honored with regular uniforms, even with the rank and title of officers. The inclusion of women in the army will affect the relationship between men and women in the whole country. It is only one change, coinciding in its results with many others. They all point toward the same goal of evolution: social and sexual equality between men and women.

Whether we like it or not, we shall have to face squarely facts that are bound to affect the postwar conditions in our country. The sexual experiences of our boys in the service were, in most instances, in contrast to their upbringing and their training in civilian life. The society which they had known offered no socially accepted form of sexual gratification, since prostitution, a token of feminine humiliation, has been socially and legally barred. Those stationed in European countries especially were exposed to considerable sexual "freedom," a practice which may make it difficult for many to return to the rather strict and Puritan customs prevailing in prewar America.

The situation confronting the women who served in the armed forces is similar in regard to new sexual patterns which arose. One cannot and should not generalize, but here, too, it is necessary to face the facts. Many of the girls, taken away from home, from the protection of their families and the strict regulations of the community, were exposed to the unceasing and insistent demands of their male companions, to the romantic lure of nature, moonlight or the tropics, to the despair of loneliness and homesickness, to a living condition where the shadow of death made life cheap and put a high value on pleasure. These girls, in their new status as soldiers, could no longer look at sex with the bashful embarrassment with which they were brought up. Living and working conditions made many of them act and feel in a more masculine fashion.

While all these changes affected men and women in service, the home front did not stand still. The scarcity of available men and the threat of sexual deprivation outweighed for many girls and women the importance of chastity and fidelity, not to speak of those girls who excused their desire for fun, for admiration and appreciation, by assuming a "patriotic duty" to satisfy the desires of the boys home on furlough. The general trend toward the loosening of sexual morals made the position of war wives and war brides even more precarious than the hardships of separation would imply. It is hard enough to be alone, lonesome, and without outlet for affections and sexual desires; it is worse to know that "he" probably found his pleasures and satisfactions in one way or another. Moreover, this had to be endured at a time when girls and women in their community enjoyed a new and fascinating freedom in their status as war workers, finding their place at the side of men in factories, in industry and technical fields which previously had been the domain of men alone. They worked as men did, they dressed like men, against all the futile protests of the frightened males who wanted to keep the women "in their place," that is, in skirts (pants always having been regarded as the symbol of masculine superiority). They made money as never before and became utterly independent of any male supporter. It is no wonder that they acted as men did in regard to sex also, choosing and demanding, no longer waiting, no longer relying passively on their attracting charms.

THE CHANGED MARITAL RELATIONSHIP

This recognition is imperative today if we wish to avoid utter confusion in our generation, faced as it is with tremendous sexual and marital conflicts. Without a clear understanding of the underlying social and moral factors, no individual problem between husband and wife or between lovers can be approached sensibly or solved at all. Men and women alike become unwilling to accept each other as they are. And the more discouraged they are, the less they can endure; and the more they demand and expect, the less they will get. Consequently the rate of divorce will probably increase significantly. The blame will be attributed to a great variety of reasons. Husbands and wives will blame each other; they will complain of their incompatibility or of unfavorable economic conditions.

It is as wrong to put the blame for the broken marriages on a lack of familiarity as on the boredom of prolonged familiarity; war marriages may as frequently break up as marriages of long standing. Little do both parties involved realize that their difficulties lie neither in their respective qualities nor in living conditions, but in their inability to find a new equilibrium between themselves as the old foundation of their relationship crumbles. Every financial or social problem challenging them brings their inner conflict into the open. They differ about the function which husband or wife should assume; they expect and demand from each other what each is unwilling and incapable of performing. The increased rate of divorce, in turn, makes men and women more sensitive and increases their demands for safeguards.

IMMORALITY VERSUS NEW MORALS

It would be unjust to label these changes as "growing immorality." It is true that war has always brought in its wake a loosening of morals. That was true after the last war, and one might consider present conditions a repetition of a temporary immorality. But this time it is more than that. There is no return to "normality" possible, because these changes reflect more than merely loose morals; they are an indication of a change in the moral values themselves, reflecting a new position of woman in society, a new relationship between man and woman, who look with new eyes upon sex in its physical and social implications, at least in the big cities. During and after World War I the sexual delinquency of young girls increased, as has happened this time again. But there is one fundamental difference: Girls arrested twenty-five years ago were fully aware of their misconduct. Today, when apprehended for similar offenses, they are defiant, denying anybody the right to interfere with their personal affairs. They maintain that they can do with their own bodies as they please. Sexual delinquency is as anti-social today as ever before and immorality exists today as it did twenty-five years ago; but it is more difficult to draw the line between decency and immorality, because the morals of the whole population are changing, and sexual patterns of today should not and cannot be compared with standards existing a quarter of a century ago, since enormous changes have taken place in the meantime.[2] There are certain sexual patterns which are condemned from the moral point of view by every present-day community; but many other sexual behavior patterns are considered "decent" by one group and "immoral" by another.

One factor makes the correct evaluation of sexual standards extremely difficult: the social conventions in our civilization are characterized by double standards in regard to sex and morals. Almost everybody behaves sexually in a way which he thinks would be unacceptable to his relatives, friends, and associates, and which he would also condemn in any one of them. In the past this double standard of overt and secret sexual patterns has been a necessary requirement of the double standard in regard to men and women. It was necessary to maintain the special privileges of man. One could boast privately about matters which could not be divulged in public. The public standards of decency were in many regards a method to keep half of mankind, namely women, under strict moral regulation (see page 52).

As women gain equality the double standard becomes senseless. Consequently, many things can be revealed today without damage to our social order. It is characteristic of our time that the University of Indiana, the Medical Division of the National Research Council, and the Medical Division of the Rockefeller Foundation are supporting a long-range research project by Dr. Alfred Kinsey to ex-

[2] "Our civilization must deal with cultural standards that go down under our eyes and new ones that arise from a shadow upon the horizon. We must be willing to take account of changing normalities, even when the question is of the morality in which we were bred." Ruth Benedict, *Patterns of Culture.* Cf. page 242.

amine the actual sexual behavior of our population in all walks of life, including many thousands of men and women of all classes, professions, and ages. This work will reveal, perhaps for the first time in human history, how people actually behave sexually. All those adhering to old traditions will probably be shocked by the reported facts. But this revelation will be only another step toward the recognition of the change in the moral concepts of our population, reflected in their actions rather than in their words.

MARITAL CONFUSION AS PART OF THE WORLD CONFUSION

The confusion on the marital front is only one aspect of the confusion characteristic of the cultural period called the postwar era. Society as a whole is confronted with political, economic, labor, religious, and racial conflicts and problems, to which we must find answers if we wish to survive. So far we feel unable to solve these problems successfully. Actually, the postwar problems are no different from the problems of the prewar and even the war era. All belong together. The war itself is the result of the same basic conflicts disturbing the peace and harmony between people and groups. What we experience so painfully is a struggle for a social equality. The conflict between husbands and wives is only one phase of this same struggle.

SOCIAL PROGRESS TOWARD EQUALITY

Indeed, equality is the most pressing problem of our times. Its significance is not limited to the relationship between men and women, although its establishment may have far-reaching effects upon the institution of marriage

251

and the structure of sex and love. Equality is the prize for which mankind is struggling today. The world is a battlefield where two forces meet: the more powerful seeking to retain their power, and the weaker seeking to gain influence. The powerful need the conviction that there always will be rulers and servants, that the world never experienced equality, and that culture and order can be maintained only by force and threat. The weaker reject this ideology. They fight for equal rights for all human beings—for the general establishment and recognition of human dignity and mutual respect and mutual assistance. They believe in the fundamental equality of human beings—an equality undisturbed by any individual, national, and racial differences.

These differences of nationality, race, and creed will always exist; but when regarded as colorful contributions to the picture of mankind, as valuable threads interwoven into human culture and history, they do not imply social or moral discrimination. Those who have no faith in human nature and wish to subdue and to regiment it are opposed to progress and try to turn back the wheel of time. They believe in the innate supremacy of man, and if they gain power, will succeed in depriving women of all the rights which they have already acquired. They believe in spanking their children, without recognizing or even sensing the deep humiliation involved. They look down on other nations and races, they scorn the masses and recognize as intelligence only their own minds. They ridicule any idea of equality as an illusion of dreamers, with no prospect of materialization. Their "realism" is powerful because they represent those who are in power.

UNIFICATION AND EQUALIZATION OF MANKIND

Human history, however, refutes their basic assumption. It is true that mankind has never experienced real equality, wherein members of a given society all have the same social status. But "progress" has always meant equalization. "Equal" is a social term and means having the same social status.

The progress of human society has always been accompanied by the expansion of groups to include new groups of people who recognized their belonging together. Mankind was first divided into families, sibs, and tribes. Every human being outside the group was an alien and had no status in the group, no "equality." Groups fused into larger units; and in the process of settling down, distinction between clans and families was finally broken down to give way to a new human organization: a regional unit based on geographical boundaries,[3] uniting within its framework members of various families and sibs as full-fledged citizens, and therefore as more or less "equals."

That was the beginning of our civilization. The groups increased from small units comprising one or a few villages to national units and finally empires, although mostly by force and conquest. The structure of all these groups remained full of inner contradictions. While human beings, bound together by common laws, were compelled to respect and accept each other, they were no longer integrated in a

[3] H. G. S. Maine (*Ancient Law;* J. Murray, London, 1906) describes the distinction between kinship and territorial ties.

253

homogeneous and close unit, as had previously existed within a clan. Members of different families, becoming fellow citizens, could no longer kill each other as they did before, but their friendship and cooperation were still limited. Short of physical destruction, they could abuse, cheat, and exploit each other. Necessity for a very subtle method of warfare and self-protection may have been one of the forces which compelled man to use his brains more than his fists. One's fellow man became a very peculiar mixture of friend and enemy. This type of human relationship, characteristic of the whole "civilized" society, invaded even the close relationship within the family.

As human culture, based on mutual exploitation, has made so little progress in respect to human interrelationships, many despair of any future progress of mankind. What, they ask, has been gained by all the development of science, by all the technical progress, if man suffers today as never before, if war ravages and threatens more violently and more destructively than in any previous time? If we compare our present civilization with that of the ancient Greeks, small indeed is the progress man has made. We must recognize, however, that even today we belong to the same cultural period as the ancient Greeks. One of the reasons why the ancient world could not develop a new social order, why mankind at this period could not progress, was its inability to eliminate the enemy *within the group*. Society at this time was a slave society and did not permit the acceptance of fundamental and equal human rights. The idea of human equality, however, had already been conceived and survived—as Christianity—the deep cultural relapse which mankind suffered during the Middle

Ages.[4] Not until the Renaissance could the cultural level of the ancient world be slowly resumed.

Since then, mankind has witnessed rapid progress. Especially was the fundamental tendency to unify accelerated when science and technology brought men closer together than they had been before. Distances shrank, and the whole civilized world became one unit, first of knowledge and art, more recently also economically, although not yet politically. Empires arose again, embracing the whole world. Today the view is widely accepted that the world is one family—the family of man. We all belong together, irrespective of color and race, of creed and culture; even irrespective of the degree of civilization. Whatever happens in one part of this earth affects all of mankind. This growing unity levels off the distinctions between human beings. The French and the Russian Revolutions ending feudalism, the Bill of Rights, and the American Civil War are milestones in the emancipation of all underprivileged groups. The idea of human rights brought recognition of the rights of laborers, children, women, and all races.

But the rise of the previously suppressed groups engendered the insidious drive of reaction. Equality, a promise to one group, is a threat to the other. As the growing equality of women intensifies and aggravates the struggle

[4] The idea of human equality was first conceived under the influence of Greek stoicism, later furthered by Roman law, and finally put into practice by the early Christians. Galatians (III, 28) speaks about the equality of man before God. Sex equality was also described by Plato and later Roman lawyers. In the fourth century A. D. the triumph of the Augustinian doctrine of predestination stopped the development of the stoic-Christian ideas of the equality of man and established the medieval orthodoxy. According to it, worldly inequality is a part of the divine scheme of things and the consequence of a fall willed by God (*Encyclopaedia of the Social Sciences,* vol. 5).

between the sexes, so, in general, emancipation provokes all those who consider their privileges endangered. Consequently, competition increases universally, and warfare in its most violent and heinous form results, threatening the whole culture and the very existence of mankind. But reaction never can win. The wheel of time never turns back, except in complete collapse. It is possible to destroy a whole culture—mankind has often experienced such destruction —but never has one stage of development been followed by a reestablishment of what had preceded. If mankind survives at all the terrific upheaval of our days, it can never be as it was before laborers, women, and all races gained social status and full citizenship. Either we shall perish, or we shall establish real equality, which is the basis of democracy. There must be a new order that will give meaning to this word so often used for a principle so little practiced.

DEMOCRATIC LIVING

It seems to be necessary at this point to examine what democracy really means. We all use this term constantly, without checking carefully its real meaning and practical implications for all of us in our home, at work, in our political and social activities. The word "democracy" has a very definite and simple meaning. It is Greek and means literally "the rule of the people." In a political democracy the people is the government. The people means you and me, means every man and every woman. Under democracy each has the status of a sovereign and should possess all the majesty, dignity, and respect that is due to a ruler. That is the meaning of democracy: respect and dignity for every citizen, be he colored or white, worker or employer, rich or poor, Jew or Gentile, woman or man.

The worst enemy of these social equalities is prejudice, be it racial, religious, social, or national. It creates a barrier between man and man, citizen and citizen, and prevents the recognition of mutual dignity and respect. It is based on fear and distrust, and hinders the development of a feeling of belonging, of the unity among citizens, without which cooperation and harmony is impossible. The battle against suppression and persecution, the fight for freedom is fought on many fronts, not only in Europe and Asia, but right here at home. Most of the battle lines are well recognized, and people have taken their places on either side of the barricade. All struggles are complicated and hard, confusing and confused. However, the parties involved know the game, and the public watches with bated breath the outcome, which is decisive for every one of us. We all know the precariously established truce between labor and management, breaking in open conflict every now and then. There is the struggle for fair employment, intended to give the colored people equal chance to work.

There is no sense in shutting our eyes to the fact that America faces a grave problem now that the war is over. The government and the people are seriously concerned with the establishment of conditions all over the world that will permit peace and prosperity for all. The plans are not merely political, concerning enemy countries and the conquered nations crippled by war and occupation. They are also economic, and they involve the whole world, including our own country. Establishment of equal human rights cannot be limited to Europe or Asia. We must either find a way to establish political, economic, and psychological conditions suitable for democracy, at home, at our very doorstep, or we shall fail to establish them anywhere in the world.

Only a few of us are aware, however, that we still have to overcome another form of discrimination, a discrimination which, directed against one whole segment of our population, reaches deep into every family and every home and is apparent in the most intimate relationship—between husband and wife, between father and mother. This struggle is especially insidious because many participants are utterly unaware that they fight, that they are in competition, and because it involves changes in this intimate and personal relationship, grown in century-old traditions. This conflict not only affects the relationship between men and women, but also disturbs the relationship between mother and daughter and disturbs friendships between girls and girls, who happen to stand on opposite sides of the fence. The full emancipation of women is necessary for the development of equal human rights. Turning back the page of time means Fascism.

The idea of equality, more and more distinguishable on the horizon, will prevent a relapse into a state of masculine dominance—regardless of how fiercely the forces of reaction may strive; regardless even of how many victories they may achieve. Nor will women, on the other hand, have the chance to become the dominant sex, either; for precisely as the tyranny of men is vain against the idea of equality, so likewise will the tyranny of women be vain. Frightened, discouraged males may temporarily succumb to the leadership of groups which, along with the suppression of women's rights, will endeavor to subdue races and creeds, and fight equality in whatever form it appears. However, those who persist in oppressing others must inevitably perish. They must constantly remain on the alert, must continually defend themselves against the suppressed, who demand their rights. No psychological or actual armament they may build for this defense will be strong enough to protect their supremacy. Fear is their reward, as their distrust in their fellow men deprives them of the essential security which man can find only in his feeling of belonging with others, in his realization of being accepted by his fellow men.

All schemings and defense mechanisms, employed by those who fight for their superiority, are incompatible with happiness and harmony—which is and was eternally the deepest desire of men, for which they worked, fought, lived, and died. The obvious trend of evolution leads to a conception of living together without force and suppression. And whoever stamps himself against evolution will perish. His memory will be swept from this earth.[5] As the conquest over nature advances, as social adjustments progress, as fewer and fewer individuals are thwarted in the satisfaction of their elementary desires, niggardliness and suspicion will operate less potently, generosity and goodwill more potently—and the strength of the idea of equality must increase.

WOMAN'S CONTRIBUTION TO PROGRESS

Where can we all, each one of us, make our contribution to the progress of mankind? Only by ourselves, in our personal relationships to others, most strongly in our own

[5] Alfred Adler, *Social Interest: A Challenge to Mankind.* G. P. Putnam's Sons, New York, 1940.

home. Women will be more ready than men to recognize the real issues in their pressing problems in the sexual and marital confusion. Men are often prevented by their pride from admitting to themselves the motivations for their attitudes and actions, more specifically, their fears of the growing equality of their opponents which include women. But woman, as the loser of the past, may more readily see the point. For this reason, it may well be that women will play a most important role in the general struggle for equality and especially in the sexual phase of our struggle for peace and harmony.

Women, as part of our society, of our economy, and of our social life must recognize their responsibility, otherwise they remain in or sink back into slavery and thereby retard the process of equalization, which is so necessary and vital for the whole world. The participation of women in politics will probably have no direct immediate influence on the political picture of our times. Women will either be progressive or reactionary, according to their upbringing, to their family conditions and their personal development. But the effects will be far-reaching if women actively participate in politics, not only as voters, but also as lawmakers. The atmosphere within our factories has changed in many regards since women moved in. The picture of our Congress would be different if men and women were represented in equal numbers. Such a change would benefit that body greatly. Wherever women have participated actively in a political struggle—as they did, for instance, in the underground movement of many countries—they have inspired, they have brought enthusiasm, and very often a common sense which is a healthy antidote for the strivings of so many men for power, prestige, and personal superiority. Men and women alike behave differently in mixed groups than when left alone to their own sex. And it is very possible that many legislative bodies would show the same improvement in their procedure as has been observed in schools after full co-education was established.

When women demand their equal political rights and become more concerned with the affairs of man, with economy, with politics, and public and civic affairs, they do not merely serve the purpose of their own sex, they serve society as a whole. It is no longer the question of proving that women can do a man's job—this proof belongs already to history. It is now a question of taking on responsibility, and not withdrawing any longer from the duties of every citizen. Whether women will gain full social and political status, and whether the forces of progress or reaction will win in this country, depends upon all of us, on our courage and determination. It depends upon whether women are merely interested in the circle of their immediate activities, or whether they have enough social interest to be concerned with the problems with which we are all confronted, simultaneously.

One reason why we can expect a healthy influence, once women have started to participate fully in public affairs, is the very fact that they were not permitted to do so in the past. People who had been subjected to discrimination, who were deprived or limited in their human rights, who felt inferior and were kept in submission, have a general tendency to become keenly aware of social relationships and sensitive to injustice. As long as they accept their fate submissively, they are an obstacle to progress. But as soon as they free themselves, they drive farther to better and healthier conditions.

TOWARD A NEW CULTURE?

It is necessary to understand this evolution toward equality, in order to visualize the future relationship between men and women. A new human relationship, based on mutual understanding and assistance, demands a deep spirit of comradeship, which alone can bring peace between men and women, with respect for each others' rights and dignity instead of fear and distrust. Progress toward mutual cooperation is blocked by disbelievers in evolution, who doubt the human capacity for complete friendliness and genuine interest. For them, love and sex will always be imbued with hostility and warfare. They not only doubt that equality between the sexes will ever be possible; they deny that man is capable of overcoming his "innate" hostility and aggression. Love without jealousy seems to them impossible; sexual interest without drive for possession unimaginable; sexual excitement without brutality unrealistic.

Are human beings psychologically and emotionally capable of genuine goodness and sincere social interest? When we regard our fellow men of today, we may be inclined to accept a pessimistic answer. But we must realize that man is today perhaps at his worst in regard to social harmony. We know that the social relationship between human beings is strained today more, perhaps, than ever before, because we are living between two stages of culture, and because we are approaching a new, never before experienced equilibrium. It is characterized by a new feeling of belonging together, based on a new conception of cooperation and equality. As social and economic demands have initiated it, so it is bound to produce new social and economic conditions, unprecedented in their implications and effects.

THE MAN OF TOMORROW

We are not left entirely to speculation about the mental, moral, intellectual man of the future. Our psychological knowledge of individuals living today permits a concrete evaluation of the actual or "innate" capacities of man. We are already in a position to answer the question of whether man is basically selfish and ruthless, regardless of his moral conscience and intellectual insight. We know facts which indicate that emotions can change, facts which confirm the faith in the future development of mankind as more than an idle dream concocted by visionaries and impractical romanticists.

Psychology and psychiatry offer an important contribution to sociological theories and conceptions. Careful analysis of individuals—especially of children—reveals a bewildering and amazing fact: that everyone, without exception, possesses hundreds of abilities, innumerable undetected talents which were never developed, often frustrated even before perceived. All the deficiencies and personal limitations which hinder personal adjustment and success are artificial, the results of a deep discouragement to which we all, as children, are subjected. Our methods of bringing up children excel those of primitive people merely in regard to knowledge and art. Many wild tribes know more

263

about emotional education [6]—education toward courage, self-confidence, and endurance—than our best educators dream of.

We teach our children culture and civilization; that is, to read and write, to count and to master many skills; but we do not teach our children how to live with others. Instead, we continually bleach courage out of them. The curse of our civilization, which turns our nearest relative into a competitor, can be studied in our nurseries, in our schools, and in our families. Potential qualities of every sort are stifled in their first gropings. Where children need assistance, they find misunderstanding and, often enough, neglect and frustration, disregard for their most basic and vital needs. Confronted with selfishness and possessiveness, how can they develop self-confidence and social interest? How innately strong must human nature be if it is possible for us to have grown up under such unfavorable conditions, against so many odds—and still to have become as civilized as we are! We have not, however, learned to mature. We look grown-up and dignified, but under a very thin crust the little child, pampered or frightened, insecure and timid, can be detected in almost everyone. Who can deny that?

In psychotherapy and child guidance we witness in individuals the emergence of qualities which without therapy and guidance never would have been developed. Children especially can suddenly commence to grow intellectually, artistically, or morally when exposed to new stimulating

---

[6] "The Samoan background which makes growing up so easy, so simple a matter, is the general casualness of the whole society." Margaret Mead, *Coming of Age in Samoa*. William Morrow and Company, New York, 1928.

and encouraging influences. It matters little that such experiences are relatively infrequent and exceptional, as only a small portion of our population has been exposed so far to psychiatric treatment; and not all so exposed respond favorably, for not always can conditions and attitudes be sufficiently changed. Nevertheless, such experiences of re-education refute the criticism that our attitude is unrealistic and our inferences over-optimistic.

Anthropology seems to provide some proof of the hidden potentialities of man. For the past 25,000 years, mankind has undergone very little change physically. Our brain is almost identical with that of the prehistoric Cromagnon, but what a difference in function! It took time and experiences to make our brain function as it does today; but the capacity existed many thousands of years ago. Several times in history this progress from a lower stage of development to one more advanced occurred abruptly. In our times, this point has been brought home unmistakably. Wild tribes living in remote parts of the world, untouched by modern civilization, remain savage, crude, and undeveloped; a wide realm of art and science separates us from them. But if one of these people is brought into our civilization, he acquires skills and develops mental capacities unimaginable in his tribe. In his natural environment no one could have anticipated such qualities and potentialities, and he would never have developed them there. Physiologically, as genotype, he is no different from his relatives still living, say, in Africa. Today, among the descendants of these "aborigines" —descendants by only a few generations—we find represented the highest intelligence attainable by mankind. They have furnished us scientists, artists, professional men and women. Even the less intelligent among them learn to read and write, arts that even their most ingenious relatives in the jungle could never have mastered. No change of brain is necessary, no alteration of innate qualities, to reach a higher level of culture. What is true of these groups is true of others.

Our children demonstrate vast possibilities of learning when they, at an early age, with little effort, master skills and abilities that would take adults years of study. It is not the fault of the children that little use is made of their intellectual, moral, and emotional potentialities, but rather of those who guide their destinies. Once Watson [7] tried vainly to promulgate full recognition of this fact; he failed because he regarded the problem only structurally, as if the child's behavior were merely responding to isolated stimulations and irritations. It takes more than the provision of mechanical stimuli to create progress. Each quality, each limitation reflects the function of the whole individual within his social group. What we lack is not merely a better technique of rearing children, but a different social spirit to evolve in them all potential qualities. The spirit which affects them for good or ill is the spirit of our society. Consequently, what they are is due more to the spirit of competition, fear, and hostility than to their inherited capacities.

If mankind ever achieves living conditions that permit social feeling and cooperation, then—and only then—will all our children, whole generations, have a fair chance to develop fully their capacities, morally and emotionally.

[7] John B. Watson, *Behaviorism*. W. W. Norton & Company, New York, 1925.

Then probably a new type of man will appear, differing from our present generations as we do from wild savage tribes. We may presume that the man of tomorrow will be characterized by greater social interest, a greater sense of responsibility, and less concern with his own pleasure and personal prestige. His intelligence may easily reach or even outgrow the mentality of the few geniuses who were capable, as individuals, of overcoming for themselves the social and cultural handicaps imposed on all. His intellectual development will probably coincide with his emotional maturity; aggressive emotions will be recognized not as "drives" of a misconstrued *nature*, but as the "tools" of a maladjusted human being. Just as our emotions change and mature during our individual lives, so probably will they change when mankind as a whole matures.

Emotions of love may then be quite different from what we experience today. Jealousy has no place when the elements of possession, aggression, and competition are removed from the relationship between men and women. Even sexual sensations may be fundamentally altered, for we know the great variety of physical and emotional reactions which even the same individual experiences when sexually stimulated. Today the feeling of familiarity and routine often stifles the sexual desire; it may lose this repressing effect.

Any prognosis about sexual licentiousness is impossible, as we are unable to visualize clearly the changed relationship of two human beings who recognize more important values and interests than their own pleasures and victories.

267

THE CHALLENGE OF MONOGAMY

Once sex is "purified" and no longer constitutes an intrusion in the human and social relationship between men and women, the eternal question will be answered—whether man is capable of monogamy, whether the nature of human beings permits or demands such a pattern. We must face the fact that although the Christian religion and consequently public opinion in Europe and America have, for the past two thousand years, scorned polygamy and demanded constancy in marital relationships, monogamy was always an exception and perhaps was never even as firmly established as it is today. Monogamy, although required, existed in name only. The dominant position of man in society gave him sexual privileges which prevented actual monogamy. As long as one sex is regarded as socially superior to the other and enjoys special rights, monogamy cannot be established. Once equality between the sexes is achieved, a unique relationship between men and women can, and probably will, develop. Only then can monogamy prove its value, only then will mankind discover whether it will enhance or restrict personal happiness and self-expression.

What we know of the psychological and emotional needs of men indicates a deep desire for monogamous ties. The close and exclusive union between two persons is probably the most intimate fusion of two human beings, as it permits the deepest and fullest feeling of belonging together. Such union is impossible, however, as long as monogamy is regarded as a duty and a moral obligation. Marriage of the future will probably be an entirely different institution—

268

an agreement between two free and equal individuals no longer threatened by the stigma of "sin" or the punishment of "law." Both will have the right to be with each other, because they choose to, and not because they are obliged. It will be a living together in which each has the right to do what he likes best, but will avoid what is not to the other's liking.

CONSTRUCTIVE ATTITUDES

In this way the big problems of the world are related to everyday problems of sex and marriage. In our most intimate relationships we face the fundamental issues of our time. The solution of each immediate problem requires the same attitudes which alone can solve social problems in general: courage and a sense of responsibility. Fear and pessimism lead to increased dangers, to oppression and force, provoking antagonism and warfare. Shifting the blame to individuals and conditions will only heighten the confusion and perplexity of the problem. But we cannot direct our courage into useful actions or take on responsibility in making decisions if we have not a clear understanding of the issues involved.[8] Political and economic progress must be supplemented by educational efforts, offsetting old concepts and attitudes toward one's fellow men. Education will have to reach husbands, wives, and their children to help them in their readjustment to new basic problems of social living. The recognition of our own power and responsibility must be brought home to all.

[8] Although the process by which new normalities are created in the next generation has never been directed systematically and constructively John Dewey considers such "social engineering" as possible, drastic a that might be. *Human Nature and Conduct.* Henry Holt & Company New York, 1922.

But we also have to realize that we are on the threshold of a new culture. The new moral concepts are in line with fundamental changes in scientific concepts. Technical progress, the mastery of nuclear energy, changing our industrial capacity and giving us unprecedented power over nature, is in line with a new social structure of our society. The labor pains which we experience, far from making us despair in progress, indicate only the deep threat to their position which the old powers sense. It will take education to make the people aware of the implications in new scientific research in all fields, in physical as well as in social sciences. All the sciences become more intensively integrated as our knowledge reaches more fundamental facts. A new picture of the universe emerges, affecting technical, social, religious, and moral concepts alike.

PEACE WITH SEX

As other elements of human relationships become more important, sex may play a different function. The sense of responsibility for each other, deepened and further developed, will make the physical union a token of spiritual unification. When we become the masters instead of the slaves of our emotions, sexuality will become a medium of expression instead of a lash, driving and torturing.

We, the living, suffering and confused as we are, are the predecessors of a future mankind, of generations more highly developed, more potent and imbued with a deeper culture. With our struggles we open the doors; in our misery we create a new world. Our attitude toward sex and toward any other social problem is our contribution in changing the world. Recognizing that, we should feel the full responsibility which we individually have for the development of the future, which is bound to the past. Our own life problems may look different if we can accept this point of view. A glimpse of that which could be may change that which is.

INDEX

Adler, Alexandra, 11
Adler, Alfred, v, vi, 33, 76, 99, 234,
  259
Adolescence, 62ff
Alcoholic, jealousy of, 143
  wife of, 174
Anthropologists, 23
Anthropology, findings of, 265
Athens, masculine hegemony in,
  22
Augustinian doctrine, 255

Baber, Ray E., 24, 26
Bachofen, J., 22
Beauty, the significance of, 72ff
Behavoriorism, 153, 266
Benedict, Ruth, 24, 29, 242, 250
Biased apperception, 152
Briffault, Robert, 23, 27
Burgess, E. W., 97

Capitalism, ascendency of, 30
Change of life, 198
Children, and early sex experiences,
  59ff
  concept of sexual role, 45, 52, 59
  fear of sex, 56
China, masculine supremacy in, 27,
  35
Chivalry, 39ff
Chosing a mate, 66ff
Christianity and equality, 53, 125,
  254
Co-education, 63
Competition, between siblings,
  229ff
  between the sexes, 41

in society, 155, 256
  with same sex, 134
  within the family, 107, 112, 218,
  235
Consciousness, 67
Controversies, settling of, 105, 109,
  111, 118, 165ff, 173, 178
Cooperation, in education, 217
  rules of, 100ff, 110
Cottrell, L. S., 97
Couvade, 48
Crete, feminine superiority in, 23
Cromagnon, 265
Cyclicity, sexual, 8ff

Deficiencies, appeal of, 80ff
Democracy, 106, 256ff
Determinism, 154
Dewey, John, 269
Distance, psychology of, 75ff
Divorce, 42, 98, 127, 193ff
Divorcee, the, 196, 248
Dominant sex, the four rights of,
  25ff

Economic difficulties, 169ff
Eddington, A. S., 151
Educational mistakes, 213
Egypt, matriarchal conditions in,
  22, 23
Emotion, function of, 4ff, 89ff, 116,
  128, 131, 143ff
Encouragement, 219, 223
Equality, between sexes, 33ff, 37,
  42, 246, 250, 268
  human, 31, 42, 53, 251ff

272

Europe, scientists in, 23
Expectations, as guide, 185

Family constellation, 228
Fascism, and masculine hegemony, 35
Fashion, and society, 70
Father, function of, 207
Faults, the role of, 116
Fear, psychology of, 4ff, 102ff
Feminine emancipation, 30ff, 41ff
   dominance, 22
   inferiority, 21
Femininity, 44
Fidelity, 124ff, 247
Freud, Sigmund, 4, 52, 76, 128
Frigidity, 161

Gallatians, 255
Geriatrics, 199
Germany, superiority of man in, 32, 35
Goals, of child's misbehavior, 255ff
Goldberg, G., 207
Greece, cultural conditions, 254
   religious prostitution in, 53
   sexual conditions, 22
   stoicism, 255

Hobbies, 180
Homosexuality, in primates, 9
   psychology of, 95
   recognition of, 87

Idealism, 153
Immorality, 249
Impotence, 161
Individual Psychology, v, vi, 9
In-laws, 165ff
Inferiority feeling, 102ff, 111, 117, 132, 135
Interpersonal communications, 66ff
   relations, 67, 106, 114, 117, 186, 188, 222, 262

Jealousy, 122ff

Kinsey, Alfred, 250

Latin countries, position of women in, 34
Lazarsfeld, Sofie, 163
Life style, vi, 69, 83, 87, 155, 227ff
Life tasks, the three, 16ff
Logic, as a weapon, 114
   of living together, 99ff
   versus psychology, 107ff, 139
Love, as emotion, 6ff
   as warfare, 31
   at first sight, 87
   definition of, 17ff
   frustration, 19ff
   function of, 15ff
Lowie, R. H., 23

Maine, Henry G., 27, 253
Malthus, Th. R., 203
Man, as hunter and soldier, 27
   provider, 171
   of future, 263ff
Marital consultation, 192
Masculine hegemony, 22
   protest, 33, 56
   superiority, 21, 30ff, 164, 169
Masculinity, 44
Maslow, A. H., 9, 25
Masturbation, 59
Materialism, 153, 157
Matriarchate, 22ff
Matter, the mental character of, 151
Mead, Margaret, 24, 264
Middle age, 254
Moebius, P. J. A., 21
Mohammedans, 26
Monogamy, 125ff, 268
More, Thomas, 245
Mother, function of, 209
Movies, 61, 62
Movie stars, 71

Napolean, 29
National Socialism against feminine equality, 23
Neurotic mechanisms, 143, 161, 192
Nietzsche, 21

273

INDEX

Pampering, 213, 221
Parenthood, 201ff
 planned, 202
Parents and children, 54, 213
 and sex, 57ff, 62
Perversions, 95
Philandering, 129
Physics, 151, 153
Plato, 245, 255
Platonic friendship, 127ff
Popenoe, Paul, 193
Psychiatric service, 192
Psychotherapy, 142, 264

Reason, versus emotion, 90ff
Recreation, 183ff
Religion, and sex, 30, 53, 64
Renaissance, 255
Resentment, fallacy of, 103ff
Roman, consuls, 110
 law, 255
Romance, function of, 12ff
Russia, position of women in, 35

Semantics, 153
Sex, as a tool, 10ff, 52, 64
 difference between human and
  animal, 7ff
 the dominant, 24ff
 the eternal puzzle, 42
 the function of, 7, 64, 204
 and religion, 53
 and society, 28, 52
Sex appeal, 73
Sexual, enlightenment, 57ff
 incompatibility, 156ff
 rights, 26, 28, 38
 role, 44
 satisfaction, 156
 traits, 44ff
Shame, 29, 53
Shoobs, N. E., 207
Sin, 52, 53, 269
Social feeling, 101ff, 109
Spanking, 215
Sparta, matriarchal conditions, 22,
 23, 27, 28
Statistical probability, 153
Suicide, frequency of, 154

Taste, 70, 75
Technique versus attitude, 121,
 156, 160
Tomboy, 45
Transvestitism, a case of, 46
Turkey, masculine supremacy, 35

United States, fashion in, 171
 interests of men, 177
 postwar period, 257
 research, 23
 status of woman, 34, 36ff

Vaerting, Mathilde and Mathias,
 23, 27
Veto, significance of, 110
Virginity, 29

Waldeyer, 21
Watson, John B., 266
Westermarck, Edward, 23
Wexberg, Erwin, 13, 64
Wolfe, W. Beran, 25, 163
Women, as domestic leaders, 174ff
 discoverers of culture, 27
 economic rights of, 26, 37, 51,
  171
 in armed forces, 36, 246
 inferiority of, 21, 210
 interest in art, 50, 177
 modesty, 28, 53
 "physiological imbecility" of, 21
 political rights, 27, 37, 260
 social position, 20ff
 social obligations of, 197ff
Woman's position in, China, 27, 35
 Crete, 23
 Egypt, 22, 23, 29
 Europe, 31, 45, 245
 Germany, 32, 35
 Greece, 22
 Latin countries, 34
 Russia, 35
 Sparta, 23, 27, 28
 Turkey, 35
 United States, 34, 36ff, 49, 246ff
World War I, 31, 35, 245
 and sexual delinquency, 249

274